SEW SWEET
HANDMADE CLOTHES
FOR GIRLS

22 Easy-to-Make Dresses, Skirts, Pants & Tops Girls Will Love

Yuki Araki

TUTTLE Publishing

Tokyo | Rutland, Vermont | Singapore

What handmade means to me

Creating clothes is like drawing pictures.

For me, it starts with a design in my head. Then I start looking
for fabric that will bring the design to life. Fabric's interesting
stuff—some of it "lives" for the first time when it is made into
clothes.

When it comes to patterned fabric, it's not the pattern itself so
much as the overall balance when viewed from afar that is the deal
breaker. For plain fabric, I look for the feeling I get from it, but the
subtle differences in color are also important. Fabric is like paint.

Just like trying to find the right balance of color on a canvas, I
try out various fabrics before hitting upon the right shade. Once
the clothing design and the fabric are right for one another, the
picture in my head is complete. Then I can take to the sewing
machine and turn the image in my mind into something real.

This is why I'm so stubborn about handmade things. Once the
image is set in my mind, it doesn't matter what anyone says—if
I can't create what's in my head I'm not satisfied. When the
clothing is made and someone is wearing it, the picture is finally
and truly complete.

I want you, too, to draw pictures the way you want—if I can
help you even a little with that, I'll be delighted.

Yuki Araki

Contents photo page/how to make it page

A question of design

My designs are a little bit sweet, and they're sized
to fit just right. There are already a lot of patterns
for simple clothes, and a lot for over-sized clothes.
That's why, instead of aiming for something that's
easy to alter or for simple shapes, I design with the
end result in mind.

I'm sure many of you are thinking that these
clothes look fiddly or difficult to make, but once
you start sewing they're actually easy. Seeing as I
personally am not into fiddly, tricky things, I've
tried to create clothes that are as easy as possible
and don't look obviously hand-made.

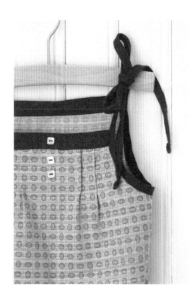

a
Camisole

Broad bias tape around the chest plus pin tucks accent this top. The bias tape is made from a different fabric from the body of the top to add color, so you can have fun creating different looks by changing the fabric.

how to make it p 38

b
A-line Skirt

This light and airy A-line skirt is made from grape colored double gauze. The subtle volume is achieved by creating three tucks below the yoke.

how to make it p 52

C
Double-layered Skirt

This skirt is made from a simple rectangle of fabric. The trick is to use lightweight material. The shirring on one side doubles the skirt's sweet appeal.

how to make it p 42

d
Mother-daughter Matching Square-neck Smocks

Using contrasting fabric for the neckline decoration adds accent to this top, and attaching it is not as difficult as you might think. I designed this smock not to be too loose, but rather to fit neatly.

how to make it p 44

e
U-neck Blouse

This is ideal for blocking out UV rays in summer. If you are making the blouse with long sleeves, I recommend balancing it out by giving it a short hem. At this short length it can be worn with both skirts and dresses.

how to make it p 48

f
A-line Skirt

This skirt is the same as the grape colored one on p 4, but made from patterned fabric. The yoke and tucks take a little bit of work, but these features combined with a dressy-looking fabric make this skirt perfect for outings.

how to make it p 52

g
Stand-collar Shirt

Adding gathers and a seam on the chest transforms this basic stand-collar shirt into something more feminine. The subtle sweetness makes a little girl even lovelier.

how to make it p 61

h

back view

Pants with Turned-up Hems

The neat waistline of these pants prevents them from becoming bulky. Have fun creating all sorts of looks by using different colored fabric on the hem turn-ups. Without the pockets, these are great for boys as well.

how to make it p 54

i

Sleeveless Dress

This dress is made by creating a longer hemline and adding decorative flaps to the yoke of the stand-collar shirt (p 10). Even in plain fabric, this looks feminine due to the sleeveless design. Adding decorative flaps to the dress-length version creates a sense of balance, so why not have a go at making them? This sleeveless design suits large patterns too, so experiment by making the same dress in all kinds of fabric.

how to make it p 57

j

Leggings in Knit Fabric

These below-knee length leggings are great for wearing with skirts, as they really give them a boost without overpowering the rest of the outfit. They're designed to be made from stretch knit fabric only, so use waffle knit or multi-layered knit material. For ankle-length leggings, see the index (p 32).

how to make it p 65

Lesson 1 Creating a Strip Placket

※For instructional purposes, contrasting thread has been used in these photos, but use thread the same color as the fabric when creating actual garments.

i̇ Sleeveless Dress

how to make it p 57

This is a lesson on how to attach the strip placket and stand collar for the sleeveless dress (p 12). ※The strip placket is attached the same way for ɡ—stand-collar shirt (p 10) and ο—shirt dress (p 22).

1. Using the instructions on p 54 as a guide, attach the gathered front and back sections of the dress to the front and back yokes respectively (if you are adding decorative flaps, sandwich them between the yoke and the front section).

2. Cut two pieces for the strip placket and attach adhesive interfacing to half of each piece.

3. Fold fabric over to conceal adhesive interfacing and iron to create fold line.

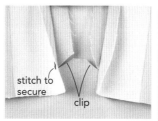

4. Match edges of placket pieces to edges of slash at center front and pin in place.

5. Stitch ⅜ in (1cm) in from edges up to about ⅜ in (1cm) from end.

6. Slash diagonally on each side of center front, starting from the end of stitching.

7. Fold placket pieces to inside.

8. Top-stitch along edges of placket.

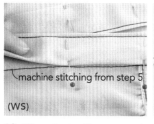
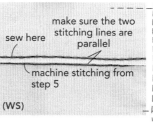

※ If you're not confident using the sewing machine on the inner side of the garment, baste placket in place first, remove pins and use the sewing machine to stitch from the outer side of the garment.

9. Fold seam allowance of placket under and pin in place.

10. When pinning, line up turned-under placket so that you can only just see the stitches made in step 5.

11. Stitch placket from inner side of garment, sewing parallel to the stitches made in step 5.

Stitch to secure near clipped sections.

16. The finished strip placket.

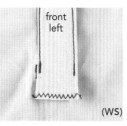

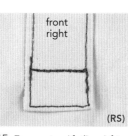

12. Fold the triangular shape created by the diagonal slashes to the inside along the dotted line.

13. Use a zigzag stitch to finish off the edge of the left placket only.

14. Layer right over left placket. Fold under edge of right placket by ¼ in (5mm) and pin in place.

15. From outer side (i.e. right placket), machine stitch in a ☐ or xx shape through to left side of placket.

Lesson 2   Attaching a Stand Collar

※After creating the strip placket, sew the dress front to the dress back at the shoulders. Finish the seam using zigzag stitch and press seam towards back.

1. Cut outer and inner collars out to the same measurements and attach adhesive interfacing to the wrong side of the outer collar only.

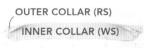

2. Match right sides of collar pieces and pin in place.

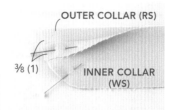

3. When pinning, fold the straight edge of the inner collar up by ⅜ in (1cm) at each end.

4. Stitch around collar ⅜ in (1cm) from edge.

※ If your machine doesn't have a measurement guide, create one by marking measurements onto Scotch tape and sticking it on to the feed plate.

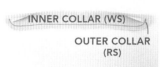

5. Completed stitching.

6. Trim seam to ¼ in (5mm).

7. Turn seams to inside and press collar into shape.

8. Match symbols on right sides of garment and outer collar and pin in place.

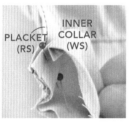

9. The trick to a perfect finish is to match the edges of the strip placket (p 14) and the collar exactly.

10. Stitch all around neckline ⅜ in (1cm) from edge.

11. Fold up seam allowance of inner collar and use it to cover neckline seam.

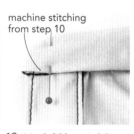

12. Match fold so stitch line from step 10 is just visible and pin in place.

13. Machine stitch parallel to stitching line from step 10 from inside of garment.

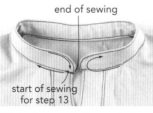

14. Machine stitch all around edge of collar.

close-up photo

OUTER COLLAR (RS)	INNER COLLAR (RS)
	machine stitching from step 10

※ If you're not confident using the sewing machine on the inner side of the garment for step 13, baste collar edge first, remove pins and use the sewing machine to stitch from the outer side of the garment.

15. Completed stand collar.

₭ Mother-daughter U-neck Tunic

The tucks at the back and the position of the yoke in this blouse flatter the figure, while the round U-neck makes it easy to wear over other clothes. It's tunic length, so you can wear it with pants, and you can even wear it as an outer layer in winter.

※ Pants are as per p 10

how to make it p 48

About my daughters

My daughters are the best of friends.
They don't look alike and their personalities are quite
different—the eldest is quiet and the second is a bit
naughty. But they always want to wear matching
outfits. Whatever I make, I make in two sizes.

I'd love to choose a different fabric and color to
suit each of my girls, but they want the color and
everything else to be "matching." Looking from one
face to the other, I can't work out which material to use.

A lot of the time, the fabric I choose is different from
their selection, and the three of us squabble over which
one to use. But even though we're arguing, those kinds
of moments are precious.

Right now, they imitate me by drawing lines on paper,
cutting out shapes and sticking them together with
Scotch tape to make clothes and cutting scrap pieces
of fabric just like me, although I'm sure the time will
come when they say "I don't want to wear your hand-
made stuff, mom!"

But I also believe that when my daughters are older and
they look back on their childhoods, the photo albums
full of pictures of them wearing hand-made clothes will
bring the same smiles to their faces as they're wearing
in the photos.

Long-sleeve Coat in Knit Fabric

The hood on this coat is just for decoration—I considered the balance of the garment and designed the cutest decorative hood to complement it, with elasticized cuffs to add a sweet touch. As it's meant to be worn over other clothes, the coat is slightly loose. Change the fabric to make it perfect for year-round wear.

how to make it p 68

♏ Camisole Dress

By simply lengthening the hem and adding a decorative skirt to the side seams, the camisole (p 4, p 30) becomes a dress that's perfect for wearing on outings. Make it in a sweet fabric for a really girly look.

how to make it p 40

♫ Leggings in Knit Fabric

Wearing skirts is a girl's special privilege, but if you're worried about them being too revealing or not warm enough in winter, these leggings are the solution. They're designed to be made in stretchy knit fabric. I made these in a dark chocolate color that's easy to match with other garments. The material I used is a multi-layered knit that is soft to the touch.

how to make it p 65

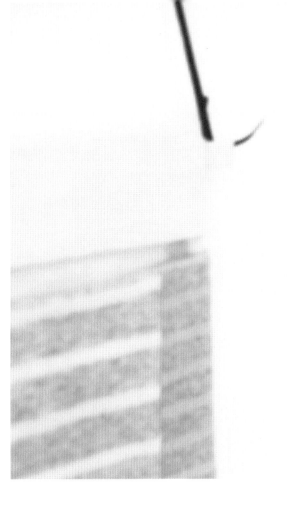

O
Shirt Dress

This dress is made by adding sleeves to the dress on p 12. Changing the fabric used for the stand-collar shirt transforms it into an elegant dress great for outings. Experiment with the choice of fabric to create everyday and more sophisticated versions of the basic dress design.

how to make it p 62

P
Two Little Bags

Although there's no zipper or buttons, the flaps close neatly on these easy-to-make bags. The flaps fit over the openings perfectly as the bags are designed like tissue cases. The pocket is made from separate fabric.

how to make it p 78

q
Neat Blouse

The careful lines of this blouse give it a grown-up look. It's designed to sit neatly on the body, so for ease of dressing, the back opens all the way down. The buttons on the front are for decoration. Details such as the little rounded collar, large tucks and gathers at the top of the sleeve combine to create elegance. This is a blouse I'd really like you to make.

how to make it p 74

r
Double-layered Skirt

Change the fabric used for the brown double-layered skirt on p 6 to create this version in simple black. The difference in length for the two layers and the hem length are what sets this skirt apart, so make sure you're spot on with the sizing.

how to make it p 42

S
Short-sleeve Blouse with Round Collar

This is the design for the long-sleeve coat (p 18) but with a little round collar and short sleeves. Spirited yet feminine, it's ideal as an extra layer in everyday outfits.

how to make it p 72

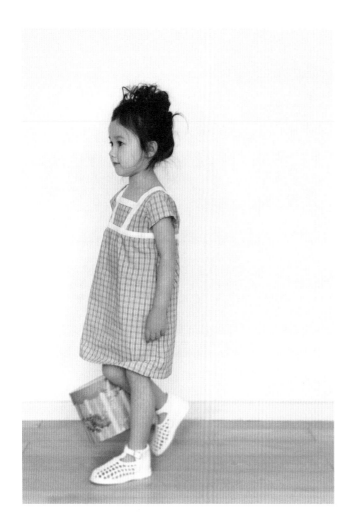

ϯ
Square-neck Dress

The hem on the Square-neck smock (p 7) has been
lengthened to transform it into a dress. In this color scheme
it has a fresh, classic look, but choose your own color
scheme depending on the desired effect. I think it will turn
out well no matter what patterned fabric is used.

how to make it p 44

The right size

Sewing patterns are usually a bit big.
It's as if to say that big serves for small too. I think it's
because if clothing is big, people think "it's fine, because
they can keep wearing it even as they grow bigger."
Small clothes seem to be "a waste, because kids grow out
of them."

The only reason I am fussy about clothes being the right
size is because they're cute. That's all.

How I see it is, when I shop for clothes, do I purposely
buy them one size bigger than I need? And if I wore
them, would they look at all good?

Children grow. That's why we should dress them in the
size that suits them right now. Hand-made clothes that
bring out how cute kids are right now—those are clothes
that are bound to be special.

u
Camisole

This is the camisole in brown shades (p 4) created in a different color scheme. The combination of cute small floral-printed cotton with linen gives it a fresh feel that the shell buttons at the front set off perfectly.

how to make it p 38

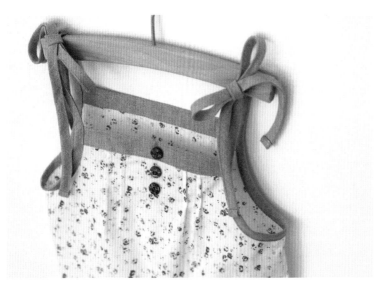

ʊ Reversible Hat

This reversible hat has a ladylike silhouette. One side is plain and the other is floral, so it can be changed to match outfits and moods.

how to make it p 63

ʊ
reversible

index

GARMENTS LISTED BY CATEGORY

how to make it

Sewing Note

[sewing my way]

When I first started sewing, I, too, wanted simple designs that were easy to make. But I wasn't satisfied with how they turned out. I'm sure that once you've sewn your second garment, you'll go from wanting something "simple and easy to make" to something that "takes a bit of effort but does the best job of showing off cuteness."

Don't put too much thought into sewing. Don't dismiss it as too much of a hassle. And just relax—as long as you're enjoying "sewing your way," you can't go wrong.

CHOOSING THE RIGHT SIZE FOR A PERFECT FIT

- The patterns in this book have been created to look cutest on children who are the sizes in the chart below. Choose the size in the chart closest to your child's and adjust sleeve lengths and hem lengths to fit.
- For hats, choose size closest to head measurement.

PLEASE NOTE: Measurements are given in both inches and metrics. The metric measurements are more accurate, and it is recommended that you use them if possible, as they will give you a more precise cut, fit and drape.

CUTTING LAYOUTS AND AMOUNT OF FABRIC REQUIRED

- The amount of materials required is listed from left to right, to fit sizes 1-2 (90)/3-4 (100)/5-6 (110)/7-8 (120).
- All cutting layouts shown in instructions are for size 3-4 (100cm) (or size M for adult sizes). Layouts may have to be altered if making other sizes.
- If number of pieces is not indicated on cutting layout, cut only one piece.
- If using printed or patterned fabric, buy extra to allow for matching patterns.
- When skirts or belts are created using only straight lines, no pattern pieces are given but measurements are printed on the cutting layout. Draft these items directly onto fabric before cutting out.

Size chart

Height	35½-36 (90)	39½-40 (100)	43½-44 (110)	47½-48 (120)
Bust	20½ (52)	21½ (54)	22 (56)	24 (60)
Waist	19½ (49)	20¼ (51)	20½ (52)	22 (54)
Hips	20½ (52)	22½ (57)	23½ (59)	25 (63)

Sewing Note

[the first step]

FABRIC

Prepare the fabric: it is vital to rinse and iron the fabric to get the grain sitting properly (ask the staff at the fabric store how you should rinse the fabric as different textiles require different handling).

PAPER PATTERN

Check which paper pattern you will need to use to create the garment and transfer markings to fabric. To do this, it's best to use paper that makes transferring markings easy, such as tracing paper or carbon paper. Once the lines for the completed garment, matching symbols and grain line are transferred to the fabric, add the seam allowance as per the instructions on the cutting layout. When adding the seam allowance, it's a good idea to use a sewing gauge, dressmaker's ruler/plotting scale, or double roulette. When cutting pattern pieces that will be finished by folding fabric edges over twice, such as sleeves, fold the edge of the material as you would to finish it, then cut out. This allows for a neat finish.

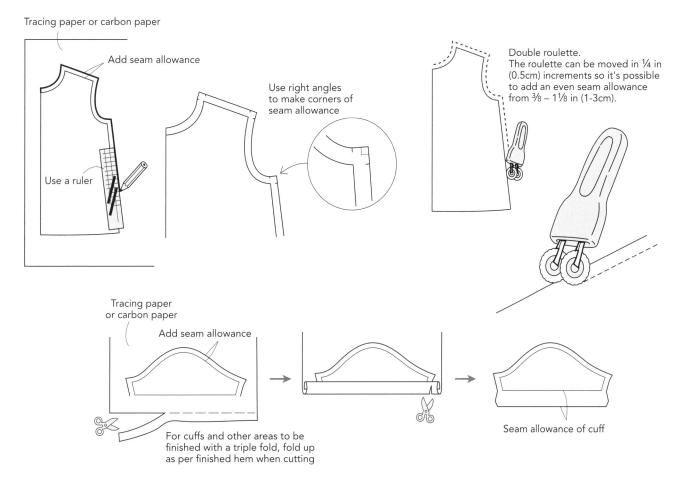

Tracing paper or carbon paper

Add seam allowance

Use a ruler

Use right angles to make corners of seam allowance

Double roulette.
The roulette can be moved in ¼ in (0.5cm) increments so it's possible to add an even seam allowance from ⅜ – 1⅛ in (1-3cm).

Tracing paper or carbon paper

Add seam allowance

For cuffs and other areas to be finished with a triple fold, fold up as per finished hem when cutting

Seam allowance of cuff

Sewing Note

CUTTING OUT AND ADHESIVE INTERFACING

Before cutting out the fabric, ensure you have enough by laying all the pattern pieces on the fabric to check whether they will fit. I recommend using a rotary cutter and a large cutting board, because you can lay all the pattern pieces on the fabric, secure them with a weight so they don't move, and cut around them. For pieces that require adhesive interfacing cut out fabric and interfacing separately and apply interfacing pieces to fabric pieces.

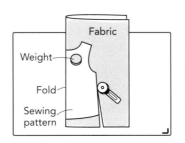

Use a weight to stabilize fabric and pattern on a large cutting board and use a rotary cutter to cut out fabric

SYMBOLS

A water soluble fabric pen or pencil is all you need for marking fabric. For matching symbols, cut a notch about ⅛ in (2mm) into the seam allowance as shown in the diagram on the right (notch method). To indicate design lines within the pattern pieces, such as positioning of pockets, tucks, buttons and so on, use an awl to leave a slight mark on the fabric. For pocket positioning, make marks on the left and right edges of where the pocket should go; for tucks, mark four points: left and right start points and left and right end points. Match right and left points and sew from start to end points at a regular width using the measurements on the sewing machine feed plate as a guide (see right). Sections that require drafting of precise lines are explained on instruction pages.

Notch

To indicate matching symbols, cut a notch about 1/16 in (2mm) into seam allowance

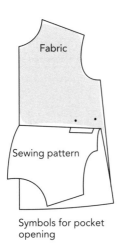

Symbols for pocket opening

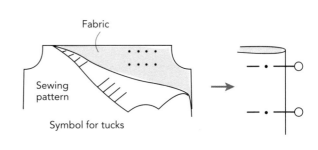

Symbol for tucks

Sewing Note

[making the next steps fun]

MARK MEASUREMENTS ON THE SEWING MACHINE

Before you start, it's crucial to mark measurements on your sewing machine. Some machines or attachments allow you to measure the distance from the needle, but if yours doesn't, stick Scotch tape to the feed plate and make markings ⅜ in (1cm) from the needle and then in half-centimeter increments up until 1⅛ in (3cm).

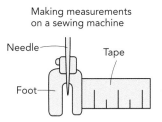

Making measurements on a sewing machine

Needle
Tape
Foot

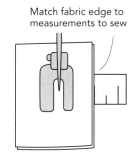

Match fabric edge to measurements to sew

SEWING

As mentioned under the "Symbols" on the facing page, I never mark in the design lines unless it's absolutely necessary. This is where the measurements on the sewing machine come in handy. To sew a seam, first match the edges of the fabric and any symbols indicated and pin them in place. Then, if the seam allowance is ⅜ in (1cm), line up the edge of the fabric at the ⅜ in (1cm) mark and make sure it keeps lining up at that point as you sew. Finish off the raw edges by sewing through all layers using zigzag stitch or a serger.

HARD-TO-SEW CURVES AND CORNERS

When sewing curves, corners and other tricky areas, wind the handle of the sewing machine by hand rather than controlling the machine with your foot. When approaching a corner, wind the handle by hand to insert the needle at the corner point, then lift the presser foot and reposition the fabric before you sew around the corner. For times when the fabric tends to stick in the machine, such as starting to sew, sewing through layers and so on, wedge a thick piece of card or fabric in under the back of the presser foot.

SEWING KNIT FABRIC

Knit fabric should only be sewn using needles, thread and adhesive interfacing especially for that purpose. Rather than pins, it's best to use clothes pegs to keep layers of fabric together. I would recommend sewing knit fabric on a 4-needle serger, but if you're using a domestic sewing machine, you can finish off straight seams by using zigzag stitch. However, the result will not be as durable as that which you would achieve using a 4-needle serger. Further, using a 3-needle serger alone will not result in a sturdy finish, but you can sew a straight seam on a domestic sewing machine and then use a 3-needle serger instead of zigzag stitch to finish off the seam. If you are using a 4-needle serger to sew a seam, use wool thread for the top threads and thread for knit fabrics for the bottom threads.

CREATING GATHERS

To create gathers, sew two parallel lines on the longest stitch length possible, then pull on either both bobbin threads or both upper threads at once. The trick to creating even gathers is, after sewing the two parallel lines of stitching, to match the gathering fabric with the fabric to which you are joining it, pinning at both edges and in the center, before pulling up the stitches. (If the section to be gathered is long, pin in between the edges and the center also). The parallel rows of stitching for gathering can be made in the seam allowance, but stitching about ⅛ in (2mm) either side of the seam line (¼ in [8mm] and ½ in [12mm] from fabric edge) creates a neater finish. Make sure you remove any remaining gathering thread after sewing.

These are my tips for saving time and making things easier so I can sew "my way." You're sure to discover your own tips for sewing "your way."

Gathering

Use longest stitch setting to stitch parallel rows ¼ in (8mm) and ½ in (12mm) from fabric edge

a, u p. 4, 30
Camisole

[materials]
※ Amount of fabric needed is listed from left to correspond to sizes 1-2 (90)/3-4 (100)/5-6 (110)/7-8 (120)

GARMENT A
• Main fabric—print in brown shades
45 in (110cm) wide—12 (30)/16 (40)/16 (40)/16 (40) in (cm)
• Trim fabric—plain dark brown
45 in (110cm) wide—16 in (40cm) for all sizes
• Decorative buttons x 3

GARMENT U (※ fabric amounts are as per Garment A)
Main fabric—small floral print
Trim fabric—plain beige
Decorative buttons x 3

★ Full size pattern pieces are on side A of the pull-out page at the end of the book

[sewing steps]
1. Fold tucks on garment front and sew from right side.
2. Attach neck trim to front and back of garment.
3. Match right sides of front and back and stitch sides. Finish seams with a serger or use zigzag stitch.
4. Join ends of bias tape to form two strips of adequate length. Attach so that bias tape seam meets garment side seam and sew continuously to form shoulder ties.
5. Fold hem up twice and stitch. Attach decorative buttons to desired position on front.

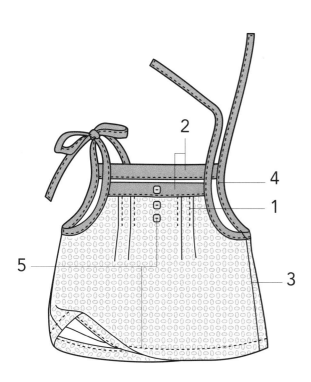

Cutting layout
Outer fabric

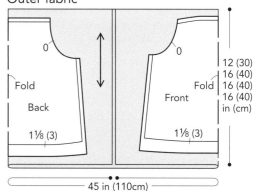

0
0
Fold
Back
Front   Fold
12 (30)
16 (40)
16 (40)
16 (40)
in (cm)
1⅛ (3)   1⅛ (3)
45 in (110cm)

Fabric for trim

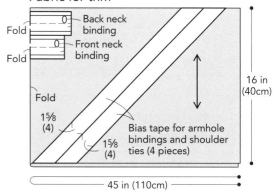

Fold — 0 — Back neck binding
Fold — 0 — Front neck binding
Fold
1⅝ (4)
1⅝ (4)
Bias tape for armhole bindings and shoulder ties (4 pieces)
16 in (40cm)
45 in (110cm)

※ Amount of fabric required is given from top down as per sizes 1-2 (90)/3-4 (100)/5-6 (110)/7-8 (120)
※ All seam allowances ⅜ in (1cm) unless otherwise indicated

1. Sew tucks

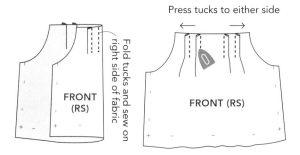

Fold tucks and sew on right side of fabric

FRONT (RS)

Press tucks to either side

FRONT (RS)

2. Attach neck binding

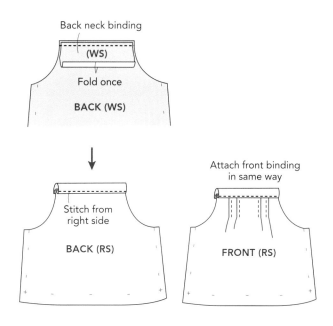

Back neck binding

(WS)

Fold once

BACK (WS)

Stitch from right side

BACK (RS)

Attach front binding in same way

FRONT (RS)

3. Sew sides

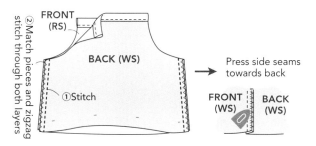

FRONT (RS)

②Match pieces and zigzag stitch through both layers

BACK (WS)

①Stitch

Press side seams towards back

FRONT (WS)   BACK (WS)

4. Attach bias tape to armholes and sew continuously to form shoulder ties

• Create bias tape

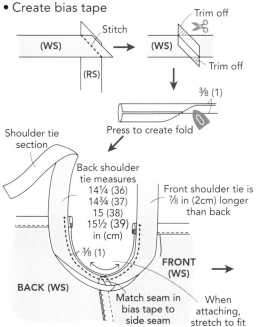

(WS)

(RS)

Stitch

Trim off

(WS)

Trim off

3/8 (1)

Press to create fold

Shoulder tie section

Back shoulder tie measures
14¼ (36)
14¾ (37)
15 (38)
15½ (39)
in (cm)

Front shoulder tie is 7/8 in (2cm) longer than back

3/8 (1)

FRONT (WS)

BACK (WS)

Match seam in bias tape to side seam

When attaching, stretch to fit

Fold once

Back shoulder tie

Front shoulder tie

3/8 (1)

BACK (RS)

FRONT (RS)

Side

Fold up twice and stitch

5. Attach decorative buttons

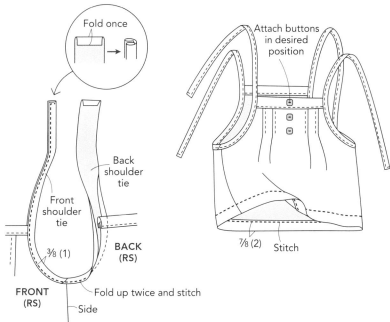

Attach buttons in desired position

7/8 (2)   Stitch

⑩ p. 20
Camisole Dress

[materials]

※ Amount of fabric needed is listed from left to correspond to sizes 1-2 (90)/3-4 (100)/5-6 (110)/7-8 (120)

• Main fabric—print in green shades 45 in (110cm) wide—32/36/40/50 in (80/90/100/120cm)

• Trim fabric—plain dark brown 45 in (110cm) wide—16/16/20/20 in (40/40/50/50cm)

★ Full size pattern pieces are on side A of the pull-out page at the end of the book

[sewing steps]

1. Sew tucks in front (see p 39).

2. Attach neck trim to front and back (see p 39).

3. Create waist ties and skirt section.

4. Baste skirt section to sides. Match right sides of front and back sections and sew.

5. Attach bias tape to armholes and sew continuously to form shoulder ties (see p 39).

6. Fold up hem twice and sew.

Cutting layout

Outer fabric

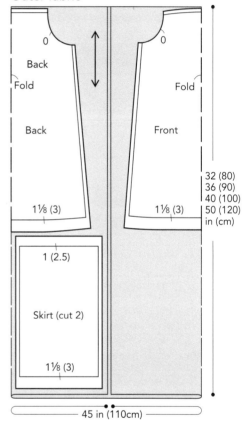

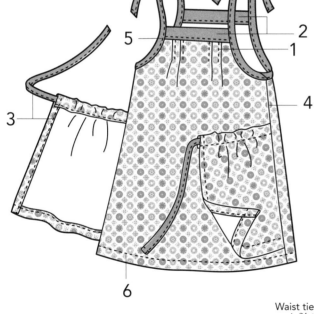

Waist tie length–2 ties each ⅜ in (1cm) wide

1-2 (90), 19½ (49cm)
3-4 (100), 19¾ (50cm)
5-6 (110), 20¼ (51cm)
7-8 (120), 20½ (52cm)

Fabric for trim

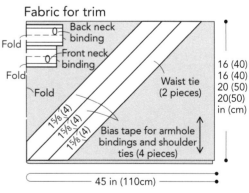

※ Amount of fabric required is given from top down as per sizes 1-2 (90)/3-4 (100)/5-6 (110)/7-8 (120)

※ All seam allowances ⅜ in (1cm) unless otherwise indicated

1. Sew tucks (see 39)

2. Attach neck binding (see 39)

3. Create waist ties and skirt

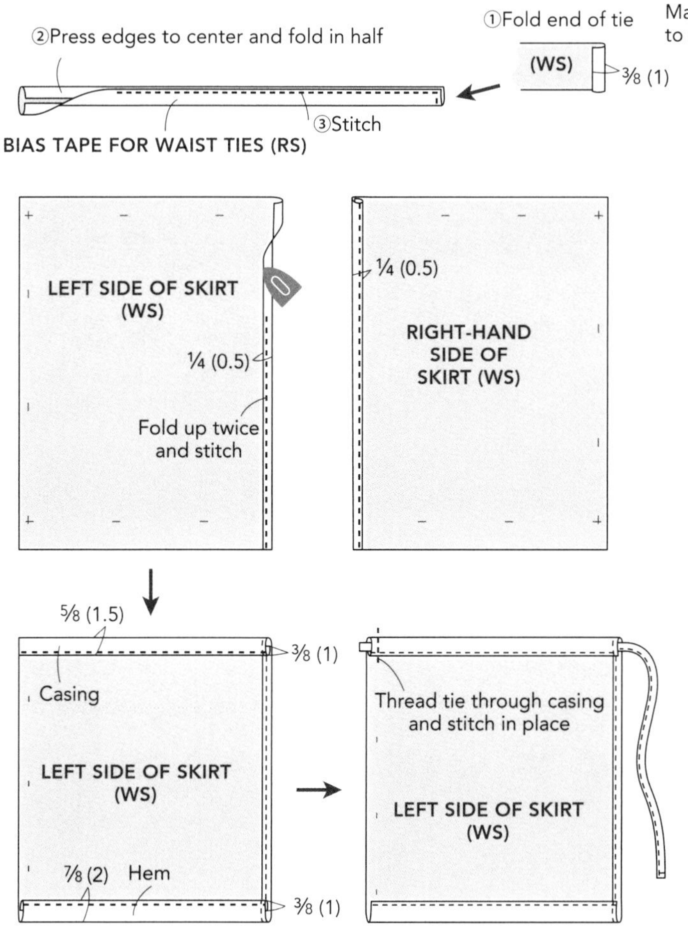

①Fold end of tie
(WS)
3⁄8 (1)
②Press edges to center and fold in half
③Stitch
BIAS TAPE FOR WAIST TIES (RS)
LEFT SIDE OF SKIRT (WS)
1⁄4 (0.5)
Fold up twice and stitch
RIGHT-HAND SIDE OF SKIRT (WS)
1⁄4 (0.5)
5⁄8 (1.5)
3⁄8 (1)
Casing
LEFT SIDE OF SKIRT (WS)
7⁄8 (2)
Hem
3⁄8 (1)
Thread tie through casing and stitch in place
LEFT SIDE OF SKIRT (WS)

※ Create right-hand side of skirt in the same way, but to mirror the left side

4. Sew sides

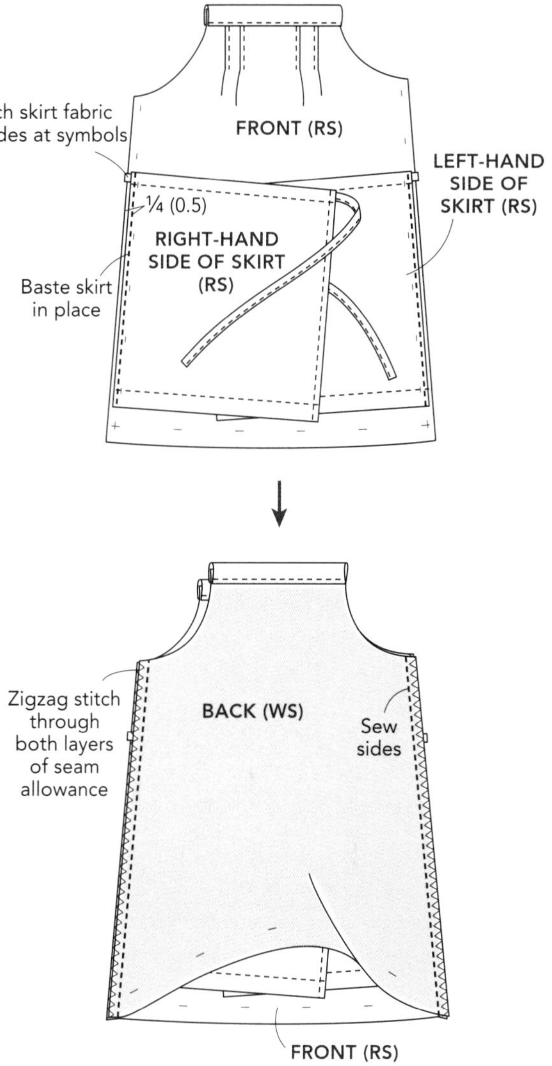

Match skirt fabric to sides at symbols
FRONT (RS)
LEFT-HAND SIDE OF SKIRT (RS)
1⁄4 (0.5)
RIGHT-HAND SIDE OF SKIRT (RS)
Baste skirt in place
Zigzag stitch through both layers of seam allowance
BACK (WS)
Sew sides
FRONT (RS)

5. Attach bias tape to armholes and sew continuously to form shoulder ties (see 39)

6. Fold hem up twice and stitch

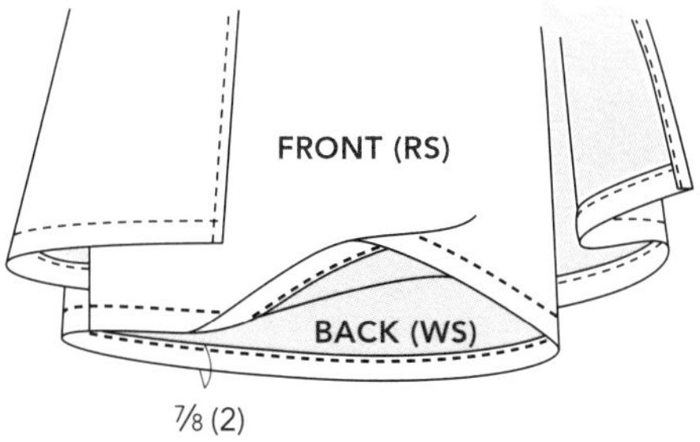

FRONT (RS)
BACK (WS)
7⁄8 (2)

C, R p. 6, 24
Double-layered Skirt

[materials]

※ Amount of fabric needed is listed from left to correspond to sizes 1-2 (90)/3-4 (100)/5-6 (110)/7-8 (120).

GARMENT C WITH RIBBON

• Main fabric (underskirt)—print in brown shades
45 in (110cm) wide—28/32/36/36 in (70/80/90/90cm)
• Other fabric (overskirt)—plain brown
45 in (110cm) wide—24/28/32/32 in (60/70/80/80cm)
• Bias tape—finished measurements 1 in (2cm) wide x 14 in (35cm)
• Ribbon ⅜ in (1cm) wide—36/40/40/50 in (90/100/100/120cm)
• Elastic 1 in (2cm) wide—17½/18½/19½/20½ in (44/46/49/52cm)

GARMENT R

• Main fabric—plain black lawn
45 in (110cm) wide—36/50/52/56 in (90/120/130/140cm)
• Elastic 1 in (2cm) wide—17½/18½/19½/20½ in (44/46/49/52cm)
• There is no pattern given for this garment. Draft directly onto fabric using instructions and measurements given.

[sewing steps]

1. Match front and back of overskirt and sew sides. Finish seams with a serger or use zigzag stitch.
2. Create underskirt in the same way.
3. Fold up hem of each skirt twice and sew. For C, attach bias tape for ribbon casing to the overskirt and insert ribbon.
4. Create waist casing. Leave opening for elastic and stitch.
5. Match waists of overskirt and underskirt and attach waist casing.
6. Insert elastic into waist casing and stitch to secure.

Garment C
Double-layered skirt (with ribbons)

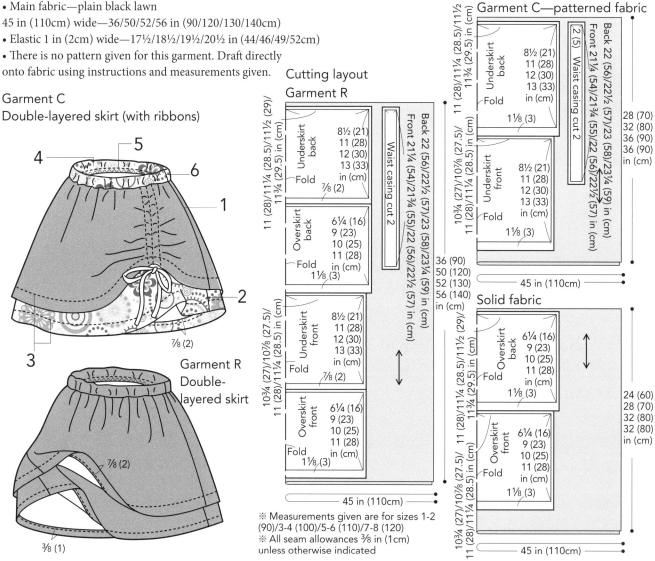

Garment R
Double-layered skirt

Cutting layout
Garment R

Cutting layout
Garment C—patterned fabric

Solid fabric

※ Measurements given are for sizes 1-2 (90)/3-4 (100)/5-6 (110)/7-8 (120)
※ All seam allowances ⅜ in (1cm) unless otherwise indicated

1. Sew back and front of overskirt together at sides

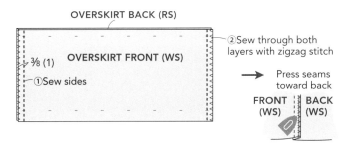

OVERSKIRT BACK (RS)

OVERSKIRT FRONT (WS)

⅜ (1)

①Sew sides

②Sew through both layers with zigzag stitch

→ Press seams toward back

FRONT (WS) BACK (WS)

2. Sew back and front of underskirt together at sides

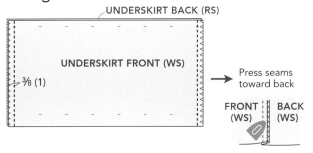

UNDERSKIRT BACK (RS)

UNDERSKIRT FRONT (WS)

⅜ (1)

→ Press seams toward back

FRONT (WS) BACK (WS)

3. Fold up hem twice and sew

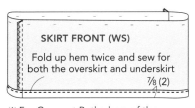

SKIRT FRONT (WS)

Fold up hem twice and sew for both the overskirt and underskirt

⅞ (2)

※ For Garment R, the hem of the underskirt should be ½ in (1cm)

4. Create waist casing

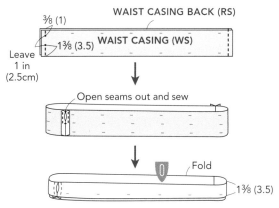

WAIST CASING BACK (RS)

⅜ (1)

1⅜ (3.5) WAIST CASING (WS)

Leave 1 in (2.5cm)

Open seams out and sew

Fold

1⅜ (3.5)

5. Attach waist casing to skirt

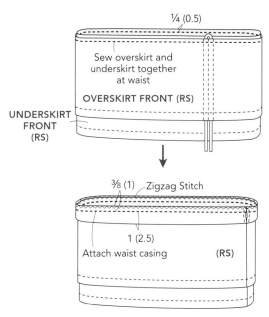

¼ (0.5)

Sew overskirt and underskirt together at waist

OVERSKIRT FRONT (RS)

UNDERSKIRT FRONT (RS)

⅜ (1) Zigzag Stitch

1 (2.5)

Attach waist casing (RS)

6. Insert elastic

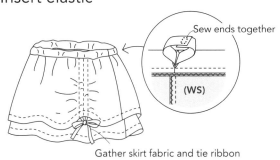

Sew ends together

(WS)

Gather skirt fabric and tie ribbon

If making skirt with ribbon, attach casing to upper skirt

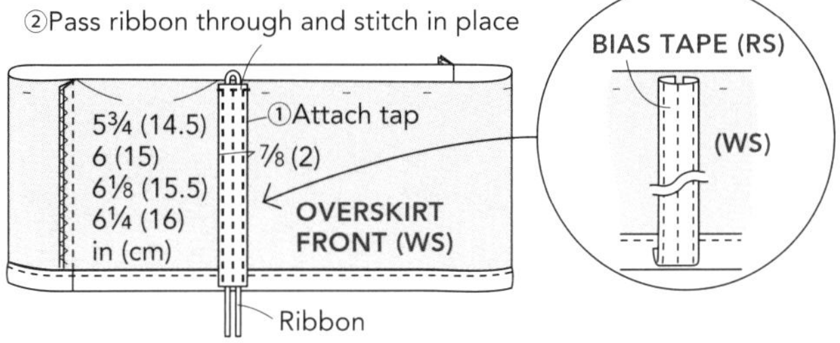

②Pass ribbon through and stitch in place

5¾ (14.5)
6 (15)
6⅛ (15.5)
6¼ (16)
in (cm)

①Attach tap

⅞ (2)

OVERSKIRT FRONT (WS)

Ribbon

BIAS TAPE (RS)

(WS)

♂,† p. 7, 28
Square-neck Smocks, Square-neck Dress

[materials]

※ Amount of fabric needed is listed from left to correspond to sizes 1-2 (90)/3-4 (100)/5-6 (110)/7-8 (120).

GARMENT D—GIRL'S SMOCK
- Main fabric—print in brown shades 45 in (110cm) wide—24/28/28/32 in (60/70/70/80cm)
- Trim fabric—plain brown 16 x 16 in (40 x 40cm)
- Adhesive interfacing—16 x 16 in (40 x 40cm)

GARMENT T—GIRL'S DRESS
- Main fabric—pale blue check 45 in (110cm) wide—32/36/36/40 in (80/90/90/100cm)
- Trim fabric—plain white 16 x 16 in (40 x 40cm)
- Adhesive interfacing—16 x 16 in (40 x 40cm)

GARMENT D—WOMAN'S SMOCK
- Main fabric—45 x 52 in (110 x 130cm)
- Trim fabric—45 x 12 in (110 x 30cm)
- Adhesive interfacing—40 x 12 in (100 x 30cm)

★ Pattern pieces for girls' garments are on side A of the pull-out page at the end of the book. Pattern pieces for women's garments in size M/L are on side B.

[sewing steps (see diagrams)]

※ Attach adhesive interfacing to front and back neck trims after cutting out fabric.

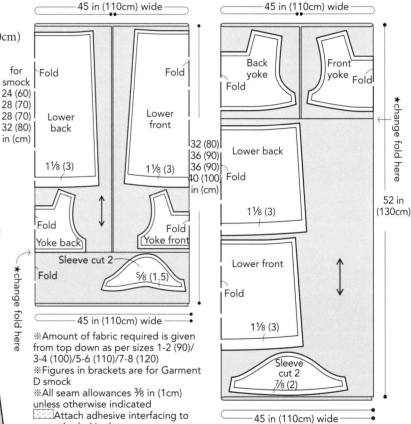

Cutting layout (for girl's garment)

Main fabric

Cutting layout (for women's garment)

Main fabric

※Amount of fabric required is given from top down as per sizes 1-2 (90)/ 3-4 (100)/5-6 (110)/7-8 (120)
※Figures in brackets are for Garment D smock
※All seam allowances ⅜ in (1cm) unless otherwise indicated
Attach adhesive interfacing to areas shaded in dots

Trim fabric for girls' sizes

Trim fabric for women's sizes

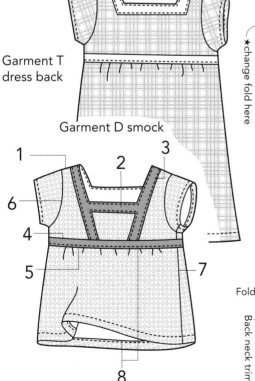

Garment T dress back

Garment D smock

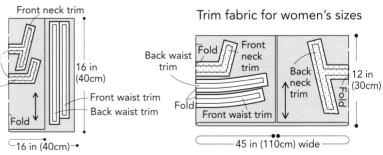

1. Sew shoulder seams of front and back yokes

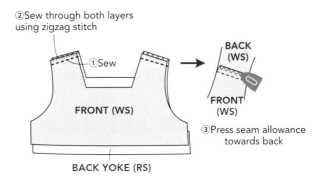

②Sew through both layers using zigzag stitch

①Sew

FRONT (WS)

BACK YOKE (RS)

BACK (WS)

FRONT (WS)

③Press seam allowance towards back

2. Create neck trim

※Mark lines in with fabric pencil to show finished outlines of neck trim

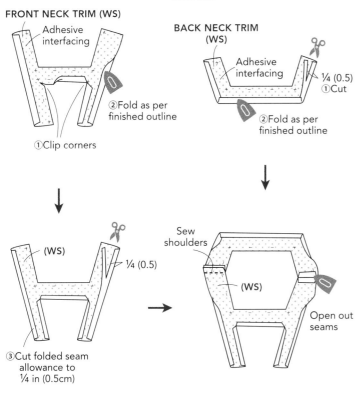

FRONT NECK TRIM (WS)

Adhesive interfacing

②Fold as per finished outline

①Clip corners

BACK NECK TRIM (WS)

Adhesive interfacing

¼ (0.5)
①Cut

②Fold as per finished outline

(WS)

¼ (0.5)

③Cut folded seam allowance to ¼ in (0.5cm)

Sew shoulders

(WS)

Open out seams

3. Attach neck trim to yoke

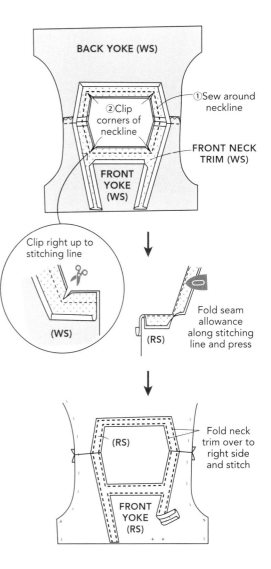

BACK YOKE (WS)

②Clip corners of neckline

①Sew around neckline

FRONT NECK TRIM (WS)

FRONT YOKE (WS)

Clip right up to stitching line

(WS)

Fold seam allowance along stitching line and press

(RS)

(RS)

Fold neck trim over to right side and stitch

FRONT YOKE (RS)

4. Attach waist trim to yoke

①Stitch

BACK WAIST TRIM (WS)

BACK YOKE (RS)

②Fold back

※ Mark position to attach waist trim using fabric pencil

FRONT WAIST TRIM (WS)

YOKE FRONT (RS)

③Machine baste

5. Sew yokes to lower sections

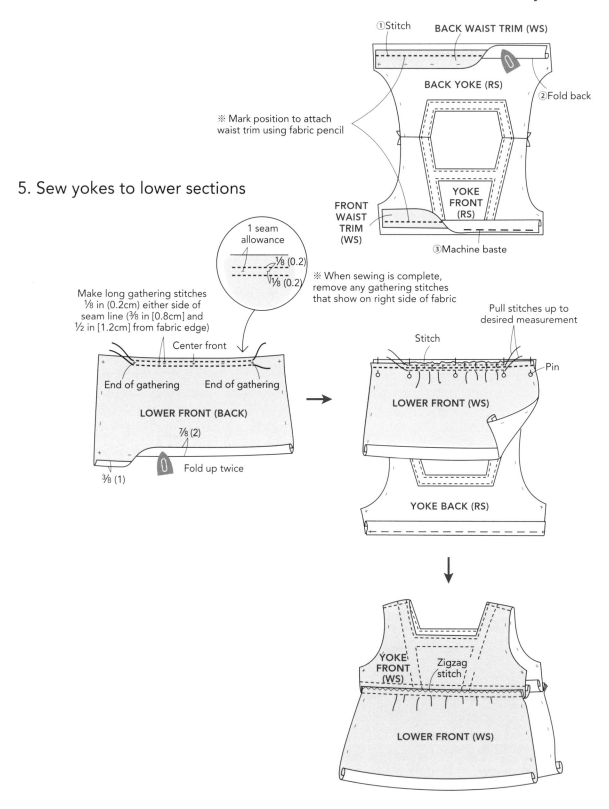

1 seam allowance

⅛ (0.2)

⅛ (0.2)

※ When sewing is complete, remove any gathering stitches that show on right side of fabric

Make long gathering stitches ⅛ in (0.2cm) either side of seam line (⅜ in [0.8cm] and ½ in [1.2cm] from fabric edge)

Center front

End of gathering

End of gathering

LOWER FRONT (BACK)

⅞ (2)

Fold up twice

⅜ (1)

Pull stitches up to desired measurement

Stitch

Pin

LOWER FRONT (WS)

YOKE BACK (RS)

YOKE FRONT (WS)

Zigzag stitch

LOWER FRONT (WS)

46

6. Sew sleeve edgings, attach sleeves to yoke

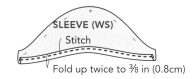

SLEEVE (WS)

Stitch

Fold up twice to ⅜ in (0.8cm)

(WS)

SLEEVE (WS)

Match symbols, pin in place and stitch

Sew through both layers using zigzag stitch

7. Match front and back, sew underside of sleeve and sides in a continuous seam

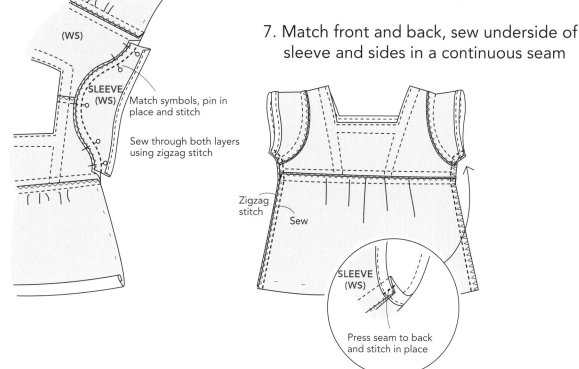

Zigzag stitch

Sew

SLEEVE (WS)

Press seam to back and stitch in place

8. Sew waist trim from right side, fold hem up twice and sew

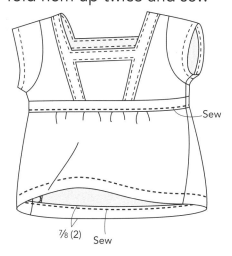

Sew

⅞ (2)

Sew

e, k

p. 8, 17

U-neck Blouse, U-neck Tunic

[materials]

※ Amount of fabric needed is listed from left to correspond to sizes 1-2 (90)/3-4 (100)/5-6 (110)/7-8 (120).

GARMENT E—GIRL'S LONG-SLEEVE SHORT BLOUSE
• Main fabric—white polka-dot voile
45 in (110cm) wide—36/40/40/45 in (90/100/100/110cm)
• Adhesive interfacing—4 x 20 in (10 x 50cm)
• Buttons, ⅝ in (13mm) diameter—4/5/5/6

GARMENT K—GIRL'S SHORT-SLEEVE TUNIC
• Main fabric—dark brown voile
45 in (110cm) wide—32/36/36/40 in (80/90/90/100cm)
• Adhesive interfacing—4 x 20 in (10 x 60cm)
• Buttons, ⅝ in (13mm) diameter—5/6/6/7

GARMENT K—WOMAN'S SHORT-SLEEVE TUNIC
• Main fabric—45 in (110cm) wide x 59 in (150cm)
• Adhesive interfacing—4 x 20 in (10 x 60cm)
• Buttons, ⅝ in (13mm) diameter—5/6 (size M/L)
★ Pattern pieces for girls' garments are on side A of the pull-out page at the end of the book. Pattern pieces for women's garments in size M/L are on side B.

[sewing steps]

※ Attach adhesive interfacing to front and back yoke facings after cutting out fabric

1. Sew front yoke to garment front.
2. Sew back yoke to garment back.
3. Sew front and back pieces together at shoulders.
4. Attach sleeves.
5. Sew undersides of sleeves and garment side seams in one continuous seam.
6. Sew hem and attach facings.
7. Attach neck and cuff trims.
8. Create buttonholes and attach buttons.

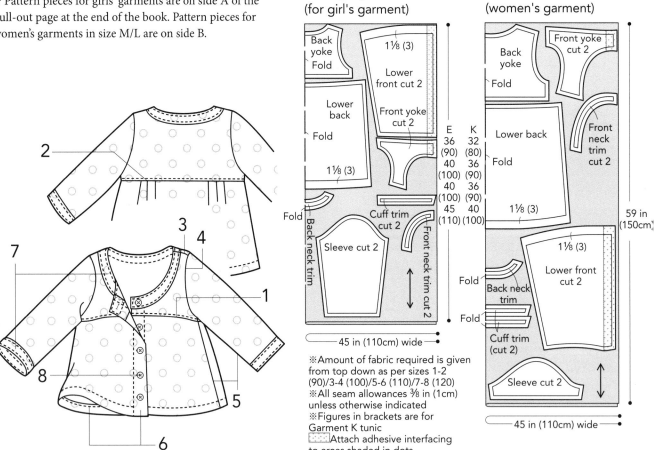

Cutting layout (for girl's garment)

E	K
36 (90)	32 (80)
40 (100)	36 (90)
40 (100)	36 (90)
45 (110)	40 (100)

45 in (110cm) wide

※Amount of fabric required is given from top down as per sizes 1-2 (90)/3-4 (100)/5-6 (110)/7-8 (120)
※All seam allowances ⅜ in (1cm) unless otherwise indicated
※Figures in brackets are for Garment K tunic
▒ Attach adhesive interfacing to areas shaded in dots

Cutting layout (women's garment)

59 in (150cm)
45 in (110cm) wide

1. Sew front yokes to front lower sections

①Sew
②Zigzag stitch

YOKE FRONT (WS)

Attach adhesive interfacing to facing

LOWER RIGHT (RS)

③Press seam towards yoke. Sew

⅛ (0.2)

(RS)

Zigzag stitch

2. Sew back yokes to back lower sections

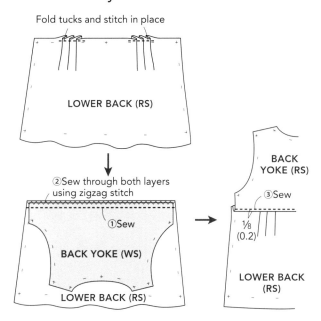

Fold tucks and stitch in place

LOWER BACK (RS)

②Sew through both layers using zigzag stitch

①Sew

BACK YOKE (WS)

LOWER BACK (RS)

BACK YOKE (RS)

③Sew

⅛ (0.2)

LOWER BACK (RS)

3. Sew shoulders

②Sew through both layers using zigzag stitch

③Press seam allowance towards back

BACK (RS)

①Sew

FRONT (WS)

FRONT (WS)

4. Attach sleeves

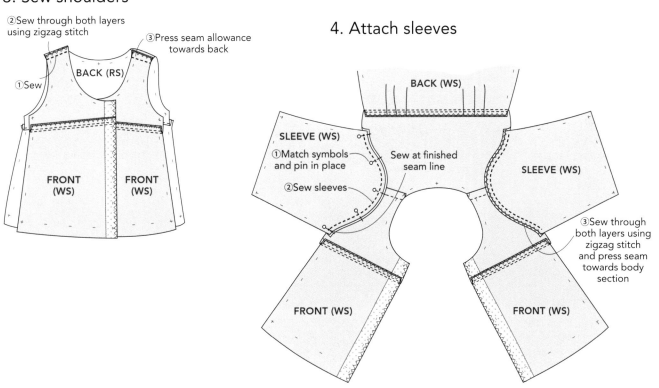

BACK (WS)

SLEEVE (WS)

①Match symbols and pin in place

②Sew sleeves

Sew at finished seam line

SLEEVE (WS)

③Sew through both layers using zigzag stitch and press seam towards body section

FRONT (WS)

FRONT (WS)

5. Sew underside of sleeves and sides in continuous seam

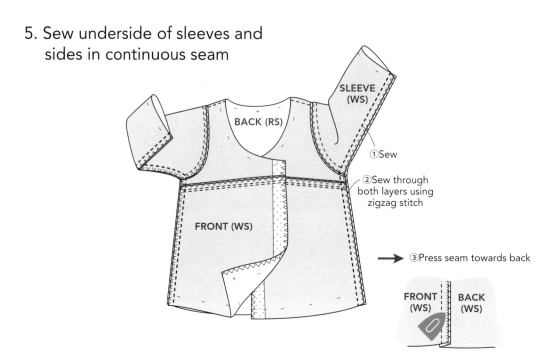

SLEEVE (WS)

BACK (RS)

①Sew

②Sew through both layers using zigzag stitch

FRONT (WS)

③Press seam towards back

FRONT (WS)   BACK (WS)

6. Sew hem, sew facings

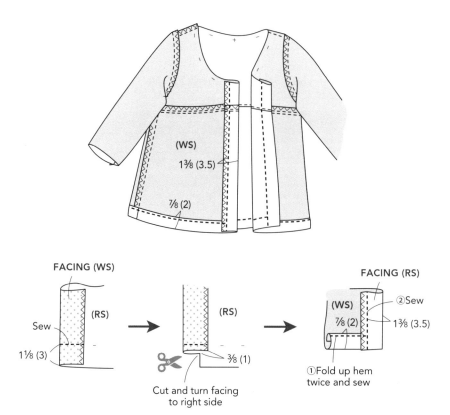

(WS)

1⅜ (3.5)

⅞ (2)

FACING (WS)

(RS)

Sew

1⅛ (3)

(RS)

⅜ (1)

Cut and turn facing to right side

FACING (RS)

②Sew

(WS)

⅞ (2)

1⅜ (3.5)

①Fold up hem twice and sew

7. Attach neck trims and cuff trims

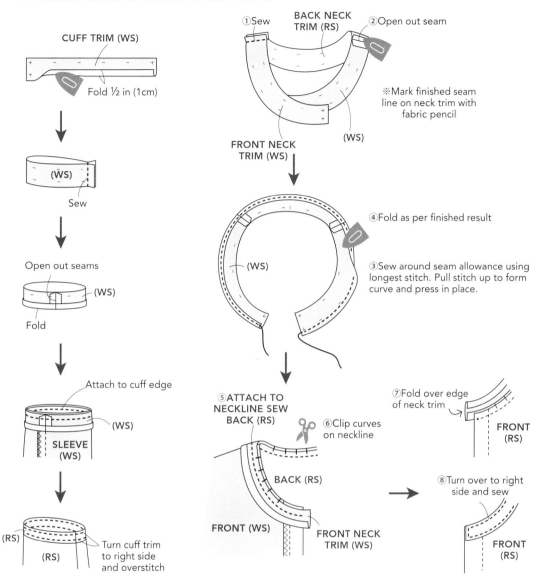

CUFF TRIM (WS)

Fold ½ in (1cm)

(WS)

Sew

Open out seams

(WS)

Fold

Attach to cuff edge

(WS)

SLEEVE (WS)

(RS)

(RS)

Turn cuff trim to right side and overstitch

①Sew

BACK NECK TRIM (RS)

②Open out seam

FRONT NECK TRIM (WS)

※Mark finished seam line on neck trim with fabric pencil

(WS)

④Fold as per finished result

(WS)

③Sew around seam allowance using longest stitch. Pull stitch up to form curve and press in place.

⑤ATTACH TO NECKLINE SEW BACK (RS)

⑥Clip curves on neckline

BACK (RS)

FRONT (WS)

FRONT NECK TRIM (WS)

⑦Fold over edge of neck trim

FRONT (RS)

⑧Turn over to right side and sew

FRONT (RS)

8. Create buttonholes, attach buttons

b,f p. 4, 8
A-line Skirt

[materials]

※ Amount of fabric needed is listed from left to correspond to sizes 1-2 (90)/3-4 (100)/5-6 (110)/7-8 (120).

GARMENT B, F

• Main fabric (Garment B)—grape colored double gauze
• Main fabric (Garment F)—floral print
45 in (110cm) wide—24/32/36/40 in (60/80/90/100cm)
• Elastic 1 in (2cm) wide 17½/18½/19½/20½ in (44/46/49/52cm)
★ Full-size pattern pieces are on side A of the pull-out page at the end of the book

[sewing steps]

1. Sew tucks in skirt front and back.
2. Sew yoke pieces to skirt pieces.
3. Match right sides of front and back and sew sides.
4. Create waist casing. Create opening for elastic.
5. Attach waist casing to yoke.
6. Fold up hem twice and sew.
7. Insert elastic into waist casing and stitch to secure.

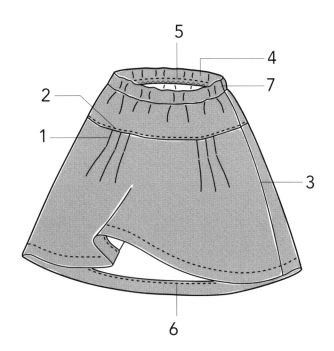

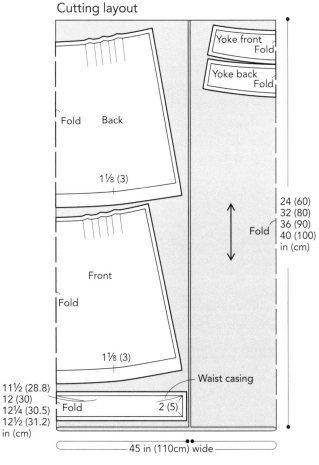

Cutting layout

Yoke front Fold
Yoke back Fold

Fold   Back

1⅛ (3)

Front

1⅛ (3)

Fold

Fold   2 (5)

Waist casing

24 (60)
32 (80)
36 (90)
40 (100)
in (cm)

11½ (28.8)
12 (30)
12¼ (30.5)
12½ (31.2)
in (cm)

─ 45 in (110cm) wide ─

※Seam allowances ⅜ in (1cm) unless otherwise indicated
※Measurements are for sizes 1-2 (90)/3-4 (100)/5-6 (110)/7-8 (120)

1. Sew tucks

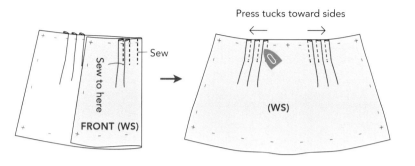

Press tucks toward sides

Sew

Sew to here

FRONT (WS)

(WS)

2. Attach yokes

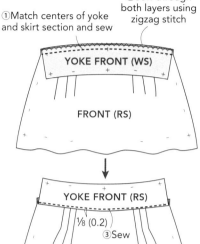

①Match centers of yoke and skirt section and sew

②Sew through both layers using zigzag stitch

YOKE FRONT (WS)

FRONT (RS)

YOKE FRONT (RS)

⅛ (0.2)

③Sew

FRONT (RS)

3. Sew sides

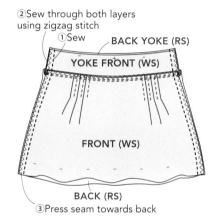

②Sew through both layers using zigzag stitch

①Sew

BACK YOKE (RS)

YOKE FRONT (WS)

FRONT (WS)

BACK (RS)

③Press seam towards back

4. Attach waist casing

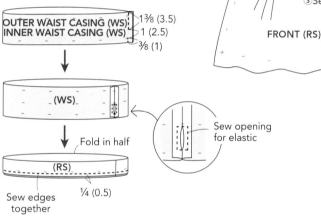

OUTER WAIST CASING (WS)   1⅜ (3.5)
INNER WAIST CASING (WS)   1 (2.5)
                           ⅜ (1)

(WS)

Sew opening for elastic

Fold in half

(RS)

¼ (0.5)

Sew edges together

5. Attach waist casing

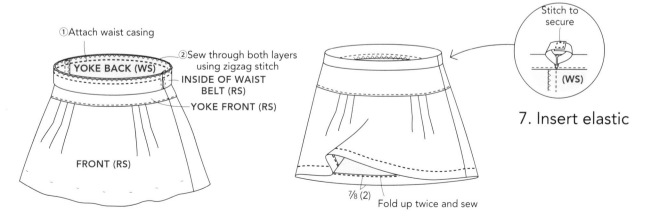

①Attach waist casing

YOKE BACK (WS)

②Sew through both layers using zigzag stitch

INSIDE OF WAIST BELT (RS)

YOKE FRONT (RS)

FRONT (RS)

6. Fold hem up twice and sew

Stitch to secure

(WS)

7. Insert elastic

⅞ (2)

Fold up twice and sew

b

p. 11, 16
Pants with Turned-up Hems

[materials]

※ Amount of fabric needed is listed from left to correspond to sizes 1-2 (90)/3-4 (100)/5-6 (110)/7-8 (120).

• Main fabric—unbleached linen double gauze twill (reversible) 45 in (110cm) wide—20/24/24/24 in (50/60/60/60cm)

• Elastic 1 in (2cm) wide—17½/18½/19½/20½ in (44/46/49/52cm)

★ Full-size pattern pieces are on side A of the pull-out page at the end of the book (※ draft waist casing and pocket binding pieces directly on to fabric using measurements given in drafting layout)

*The yoke, hem turn-ups and waist casing are made with the wrong side of the reversible fabric facing out, but you can use any kind of fabric you like for these pieces.

[sewing steps]

1. Sew crotch sections of front together. Repeat for back.

2. Attach yoke pieces to pants front and back. Press seams toward yokes and stitch from right side of fabric.

3. Create pockets and attach to pants back.

4. Match right sides of front and back together and sew side seams and inner leg seams. Finish seams with a serger or using zigzag stitch and press toward back.

5. Sew hem turn-up sections and attach to hem of pants.

6. Attach waist casing, insert elastic and stitch to secure (see p 53).

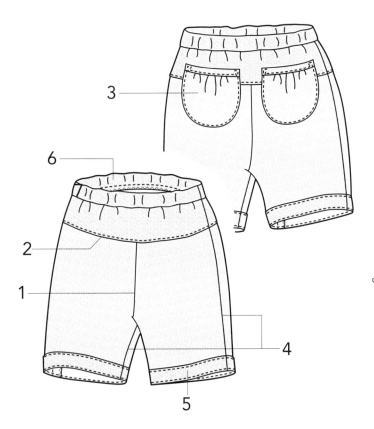

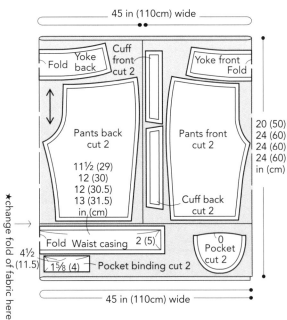

Cutting layout

※Seam allowances ⅜ in (1cm) unless otherwise indicated
※Measurements are for sizes 1-2 (90)/3-4 (100)/5-6 (110)/ 7-8 (120)

1. Sew crotch

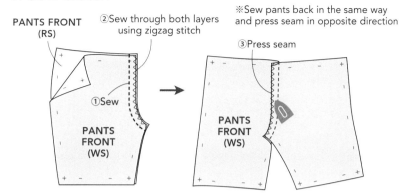

PANTS FRONT (RS)

②Sew through both layers using zigzag stitch

※Sew pants back in the same way and press seam in opposite direction

③Press seam

①Sew

PANTS FRONT (WS)

PANTS FRONT (WS)

2. Attach yoke

★For reversible fabric, use wrong side as right side

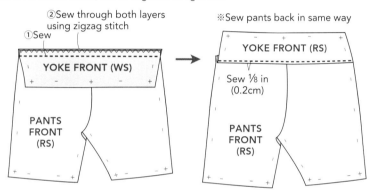

②Sew through both layers using zigzag stitch

①Sew

YOKE FRONT (WS)

PANTS FRONT (RS)

※Sew pants back in same way

YOKE FRONT (RS)

Sew ⅛ in (0.2cm)

PANTS FRONT (RS)

3. Create pockets and attach to back

How to make pockets

Stitch loosely around edge and pull up thread to fit around pattern piece

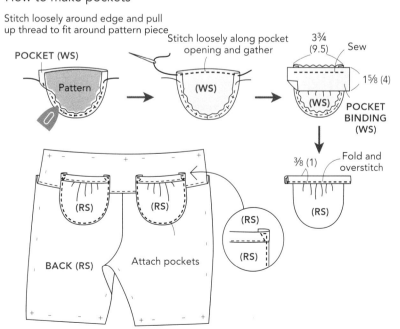

POCKET (WS)

Pattern

Stitch loosely along pocket opening and gather

(WS)

3¾ (9.5)

Sew

1⅝ (4)

(WS)

POCKET BINDING (WS)

⅜ (1)

Fold and overstitch

(RS)

(RS)

(RS)

(RS)

BACK (RS)

Attach pockets

4. Sew sides, sew inside leg seams

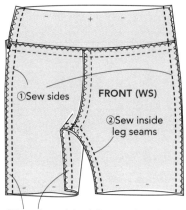

①Sew sides

FRONT (WS)

②Sew inside leg seams

③Sew through both layers using zigzag stitch, press side seam allowance and inside leg seam allowance towards back

5. Attach cuff trim

★Use wrong side of reversible fabric as right side

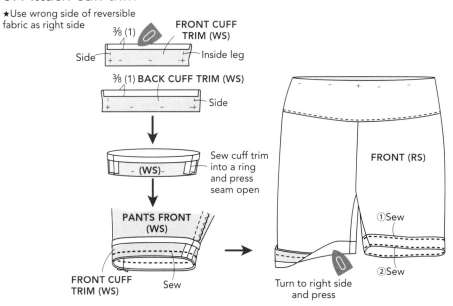

⅜ (1)

FRONT CUFF TRIM (WS)

Side — Inside leg

⅜ (1) BACK CUFF TRIM (WS)

Side

Sew cuff trim into a ring and press seam open

(WS)

PANTS FRONT (WS)

FRONT CUFF TRIM (WS)   Sew

FRONT (RS)

①Sew

②Sew

Turn to right side and press

6. Attach waist casing and insert elastic (see p 53)

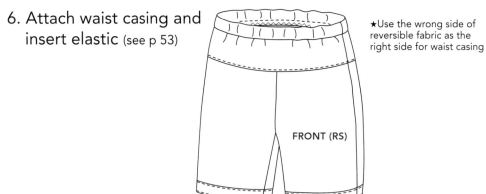

★Use the wrong side of reversible fabric as the right side for waist casing

FRONT (RS)

p. 12
Sleeveless Dress

[materials]

※ Amount of fabric needed is listed from left to correspond to sizes 1-2 (90)/3-4 (100)/5-6 (110)/7-8 (120).

• Main fabric—plain pale pink
45 in (110cm) wide—32/32/36/36 in (80/80/90/90cm)
• Adhesive interfacing—12 x 12 in (30 x 30cm)
• Buttons, ⅝ in (13mm) diameter—4/4/5/5

★ Full-size pattern pieces are on side B of the pull-out page at the end of the book

[sewing steps]

★ Attach adhesive interfacing to wrong sides of outer collar, one side of strip placket, flaps and armhole facings after cutting out fabric

1. Create flaps and baste to yoke fronts.
2. Create gathering in front and back.
3. Attach yokes to front and back.
4. Attach strip placket to front opening (see p 14).
5. Sew shoulder seams.
6. Create collar and attach (see p 15).
7. Attach facings to armholes.
8. Sew side seams, including armhole facings.
9. Fold hem up twice and sew.
10. Create buttonholes and attach buttons.

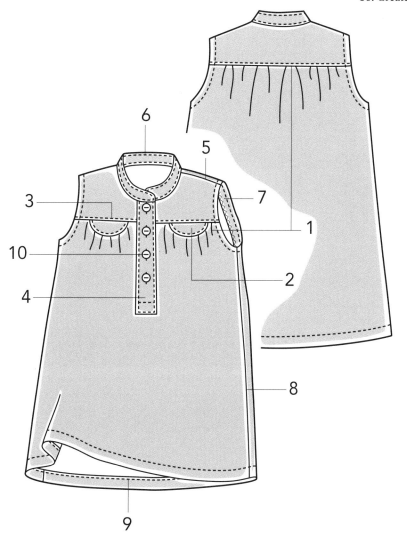

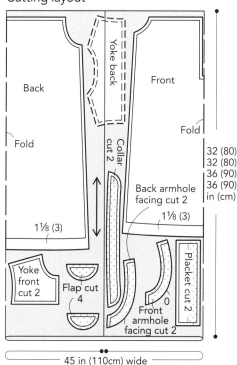

Cutting layout

32 (80)
32 (80)
36 (90)
36 (90)
in (cm)

45 in (110cm) wide

※Amount of fabric required is given from top down as per sizes 1-2 (90)/3-4 (100)/5-6 (110)/7-8 (120)
※Seam allowances ⅜ in (1cm) unless otherwise indicated
▨ Attach adhesive interfacing to areas shaded in dots, attach interfacing to outer piece of collar and outer two pieces of flaps

1. Create flaps and attach to yoke fronts

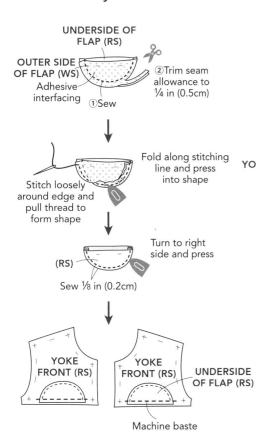

UNDERSIDE OF FLAP (RS)

OUTER SIDE OF FLAP (WS)
Adhesive interfacing
①Sew
②Trim seam allowance to ¼ in (0.5cm)

Stitch loosely around edge and pull thread to form shape

Fold along stitching line and press into shape

(RS)
Sew ⅛ in (0.2cm)

Turn to right side and press

YOKE FRONT (RS)

YOKE FRONT (RS)

UNDERSIDE OF FLAP (RS)

Machine baste

2. Create gathering on body sections

Use long machine stitches to gather (see p 37)

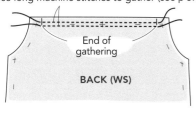

End of gathering

BACK (WS)

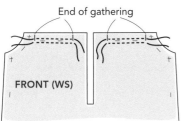

End of gathering

FRONT (WS)

3. Attach yoke

(How to attach yoke back)

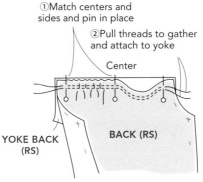

①Match centers and sides and pin in place

②Pull threads to gather and attach to yoke

Center

YOKE BACK (RS)

BACK (RS)

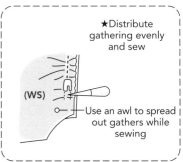

※Remove any gathering stitches on the right side of garment

★Distribute gathering evenly and sew

(WS)

Use an awl to spread out gathers while sewing

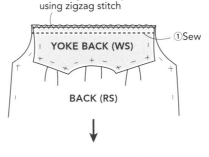

②Sew through both layers using zigzag stitch

YOKE BACK (WS)

①Sew

BACK (RS)

Press seam towards yoke and stitch from right side

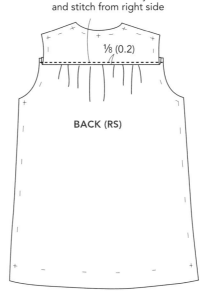

⅛ (0.2)

BACK (RS)

(How to attach yoke front)

Attach in same way as yoke back

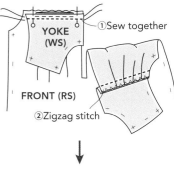

YOKE (WS)

①Sew together

FRONT (RS)

②Zigzag stitch

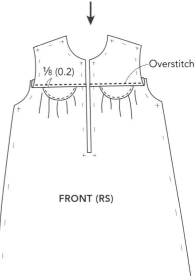

⅛ (0.2)

Overstitch

FRONT (RS)

4. Sew front opening (see p 14)

5. Sew shoulders

②Sew through both layers
using zigzag stitch

①Sew

③Press seam
towards back

FRONT
(RS)

BACK (WS)

6. Create collar and attach (see p 15)

7. Attach facings to armholes

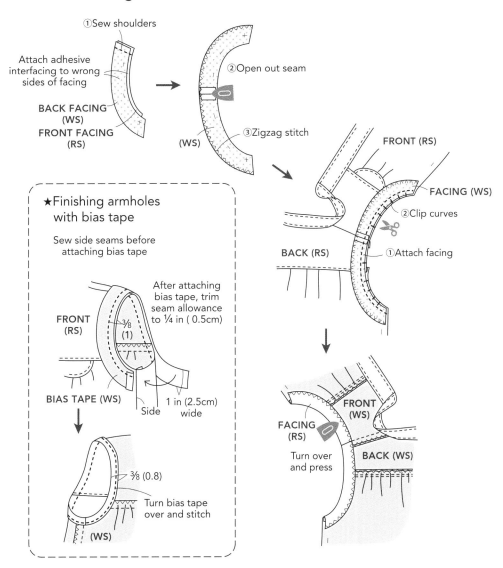

①Sew shoulders

Attach adhesive
interfacing to wrong
sides of facing

BACK FACING
(WS)

FRONT FACING
(RS)

②Open out seam

③Zigzag stitch

(WS)

FRONT (RS)

FACING (WS)

②Clip curves

①Attach facing

BACK (RS)

★Finishing armholes
with bias tape

Sew side seams before
attaching bias tape

FRONT
(RS)

³⁄₈
(1)

After attaching
bias tape, trim
seam allowance
to ¼ in (0.5cm)

BIAS TAPE (WS)

Side

1 in (2.5cm)
wide

³⁄₈ (0.8)

Turn bias tape
over and stitch

(WS)

FRONT
(WS)

FACING
(RS)

Turn over
and press

BACK (WS)

8. Sew sides

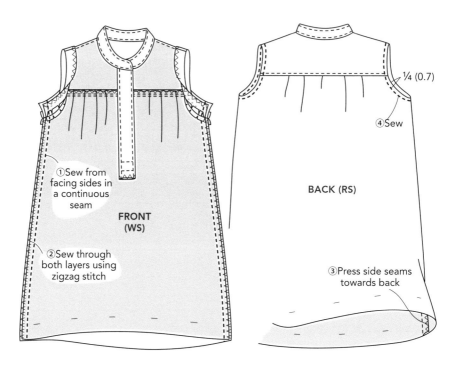

① Sew from facing sides in a continuous seam

② Sew through both layers using zigzag stitch

FRONT (WS)

BACK (RS)

¼ (0.7)

④ Sew

③ Press side seams towards back

9. Sew hem

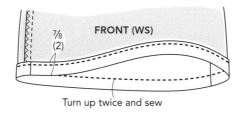

FRONT (WS)

⅞ (2)

Turn up twice and sew

10. Create buttonholes and attach buttons

ℊ p. 11
Stand-collar Shirt

[materials]

※ Amount of fabric needed is listed from left to correspond to sizes 1-2 (90)/3-4 (100)/5-6 (110)/7-8 (120).

• Main fabric—Navy polka-dot double gauze
45 in (110cm) wide—24 in (60cm) for all sizes

• Trim fabric—unbleached pure linen 16 x 16 in (40 x 40cm)

• Adhesive interfacing—12 x 12 in (30 x 30cm)

• Buttons, ⅝ in (13mm) diameter—4/4/5/5

★ Full-size pattern pieces are on side B of the pull-out page at the end of book

[sewing steps]

★ Attach adhesive interfacing to wrong sides of outer collar and one side of strip placket after cutting out fabric

1. Create gathering in front and back pieces (see p 58).
2. Attach yokes to body pieces (see p 58).
3. Attach strip placket to front opening (see p 14).
4. Sew shoulder seams. Finish seam using zigzag stitch.
5. Create collar and attach to neckline (see p 15).
6. Attach sleeves (see p 49).
7. Sew underside of sleeves and sides in a continuous seam (see p 50).
8. Attach cuff trims to cuffs (see p 51).
9. Fold up hem twice and sew.
10. Create buttonholes and attach buttons.

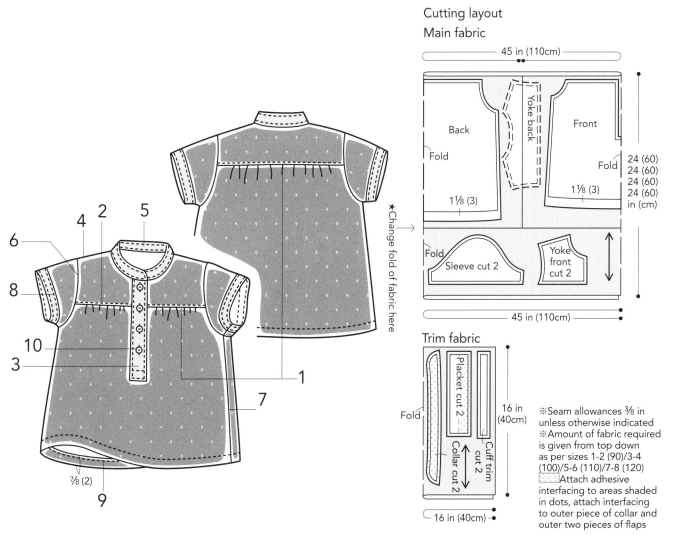

Cutting layout
Main fabric

45 in (110cm)

Back — Fold
Yoke back
Front — Fold

1⅛ (3)
1⅛ (3)

24 (60)
24 (60)
24 (60)
24 (60)
in (cm)

★Change fold of fabric here

Fold
Sleeve cut 2

Yoke front cut 2

45 in (110cm)

Trim fabric

Fold
Placket cut 2
Collar cut 2
Cuff trim cut 2

16 in (40cm)

16 in (40cm)

※Seam allowances ⅜ in unless otherwise indicated
※Amount of fabric required is given from top down as per sizes 1-2 (90)/3-4 (100)/5-6 (110)/7-8 (120)
▨ Attach adhesive interfacing to areas shaded in dots, attach interfacing to outer piece of collar and outer two pieces of flaps

⅞ (2)

O
p. 22
Shirt Dress

[materials]

※ Amount of fabric needed is listed from left to correspond to sizes 1-2 (90)/3-4 (100)/5-6 (110)/7-8 (120).

• Main fabric—dark brown check
45 in (110cm) wide—36/40/45/50 in (90/100/110/120cm)

• Trim fabric—plain white 16 x 16 in (40 x 40cm)

• Adhesive interfacing—12 x 12 in (30 x 30cm)

• Buttons,⅝ in (13mm) diameter—4/4/5/5

★ Full-size pattern pieces are on side B of the pull-out page at the end of the book

[sewing steps as per p. 61]

★ For step 2, create flaps and attach to front yoke (see p 58) before attaching yoke to body front.

Cutting layout
Main fabric

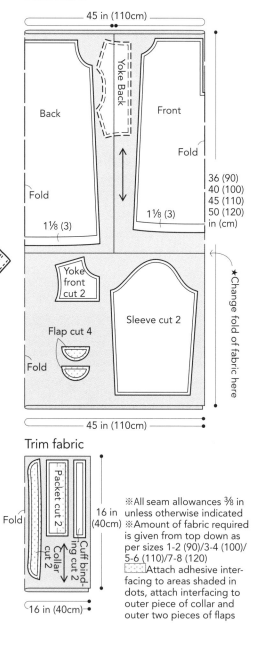

45 in (110cm)

Yoke Back

Back

Front

Fold

Fold

1⅛ (3)

1⅛ (3)

36 (90)
40 (100)
45 (110)
50 (120)
in (cm)

★Change fold of fabric here

Yoke front cut 2

Sleeve cut 2

Flap cut 4

Fold

45 in (110cm)

Trim fabric

Fold

Packet cut 2

Cuff binding cut 2

Collar cut 2

16 in (40cm)

16 in (40cm)

※All seam allowances ⅜ in unless otherwise indicated
※Amount of fabric required is given from top down as per sizes 1-2 (90)/3-4 (100)/5-6 (110)/7-8 (120)

Attach adhesive interfacing to areas shaded in dots, attach interfacing to outer piece of collar and outer two pieces of flaps

ʊ p. 31
Reversible Hat

[materials] (fabric size is same for all)

※ Hat sizes are S-20/M-21/L-22 inches (50/52/54 cm)
• Main fabric—unbleached pure linen
• Lining—floral print
45 x 12 in (110 x 30cm) for each
• Adhesive interfacing—36 x 12 in (90 x 30cm)
• Leather cord ⅛ in (3mm wide)—green, brown x 39½ in (1m) each
★ Full-size pattern pieces are on side A of the pull-out page at the end of the book

[sewing steps]

★ Attach adhesive interfacing to wrong side of the top, side and brim pieces of the main fabric before sewing.
1. Sew sides of main fabric together to form a ring.
2. Attach top to sides.
3. Sew brim pieces together to form a ring.
4. Sew sides to brim.
5. Sew lining pieces as per steps 1-4.
6. Match right sides of main fabric and lining fabric and sew together at outer edge of brim, leaving a section to turn hat through.
7. Wind leather cord around hat and tie to secure.

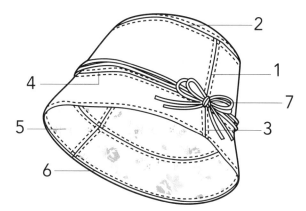

1. Sew sides of main fabric into a ring

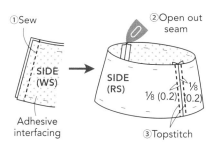

①Sew
②Open out seam
SIDE (WS)
SIDE (RS)
⅛ (0.2) ⅛ (0.2)
Adhesive interfacing
③Topstitch

2. Sew top to sides

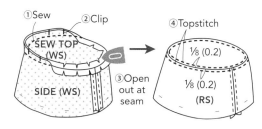

①Sew ②Clip ④Topstitch
SEW TOP (WS)
⅛ (0.2)
③Open out at seam
SIDE (WS)
⅛ (0.2)
(RS)

Main fabric • Fabric lining

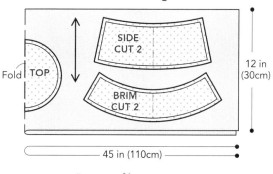

SIDE CUT 2
Fold TOP
BRIM CUT 2
12 in (30cm)
45 in (110cm)

※ All seam allowances ⅜ in (1cm)
▨ Attach adhesive interfacing to wrong sides of main fabric as per areas shaded in dots

3. Create brim as per sides

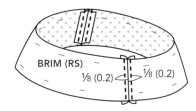

BRIM (RS)
⅛ (0.2) ⅛ (0.2)

4. Sew sides and brim together

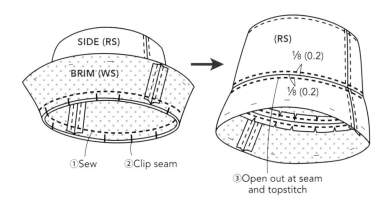

SIDE (RS)
BRIM (WS)
①Sew ②Clip seam

(RS)
⅛ (0.2)
⅛ (0.2)
③Open out at seam and topstitch

5. Create lining as per steps 1-4

6. Match main fabric and lining and sew brim

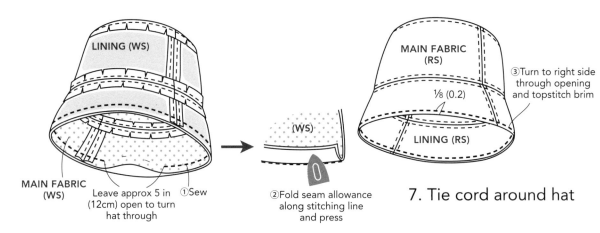

LINING (WS)

MAIN FABRIC (WS)
Leave approx 5 in (12cm) open to turn hat through ①Sew

(WS)
②Fold seam allowance along stitching line and press

MAIN FABRIC (RS)
③Turn to right side through opening and topstitch brim
⅛ (0.2)
LINING (RS)

7. Tie cord around hat

J, N p. 13, 20
Leggings in Knit Fabric

[materials]

※ Amount of fabric needed is listed from left to correspond to sizes 1-2 (90)/3-4 (100)/5-6 (110)/ 7-8 (120).

• Use needle and thread specifically for knits (see p 37)

GARMENT J— SHORT LEGGINGS

• Main fabric—small floral patterned waffle knit 45 in (110cm)—16/16/20/20 in (40/40/50/50cm)

• Other fabric—plain knit (ribbing) 45 in (110cm) wide —24 x 6 in (60 x 15cm) (for all sizes)

GARMENT N—LONG LEGGINGS

• Main fabric—dark brown knit (double-layered) 45 in (110cm) wide—24/28/28/32 in (60/70/70/80cm)

• Elastic 1 in (2cm) wide—17½/18½/19½/20½ in (44/46/49/52cm)

• Lace 1 in (2cm) wide—4 in (10cm)

★ Full-size pattern pieces are on side A of the pull-out page at the end of the book (※draft cuffs of leggings directly onto fabric as per measurements in cutting layout)

※ For Garment J, only the "short" length leggings in size 1-2 (90cm) are above the knee.

[sewing steps]

1. Sew side seams and inner leg seams.

2. Match right sides of left and right legs and sew crotch seam, leaving an opening at the back for elastic.

3. Create opening for elastic. Fold waist over twice and sew.

4. Sew ribbing for cuffs and attach to pants. For long pants, attach lace over ribbing seam and sew from right side.

5. Insert elastic into waist casing and stitch to secure.

Cutting layout
Short pants
Main fabric

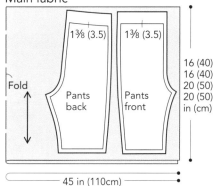

1⅜ (3.5) 1⅜ (3.5)

16 (40)
16 (40)
20 (50)
20 (50)
in (cm)

Fold

Pants back Pants front

45 in (110cm)

Short pants
Cuff fabric

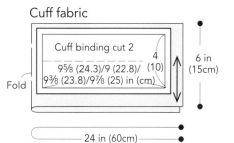

Cuff binding cut 2
9⅝ (24.3)/9 (22.8)/
9⅜ (23.8)/9⅞ (25) in (cm)

4 (10)

Fold

6 in (15cm)

24 in (60cm)

Long pants

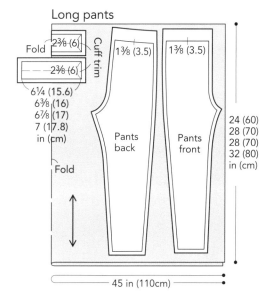

Fold 2⅜ (6) Cuff trim

2⅜ (6)

1⅜ (3.5) 1⅜ (3.5)

6¼ (15.6)
6⅜ (16)
6⅞ (17)
7 (17.8)
in (cm)

Pants back Pants front

Fold

24 (60)
28 (70)
28 (70)
32 (80)
in (cm)

45 in (110cm)

※All seam allowances ⅜ in (1cm) unless otherwise indicated
▨ Measurements given are for sizes 1-2 (90)/3-4 (100)/5-6 (110)/7-8 (120)

Garment J short pants

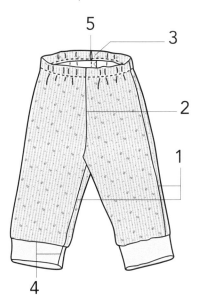

5
3
2
1
4

Garment N long pants

1. Sew pants front and back together at sides and inside legs

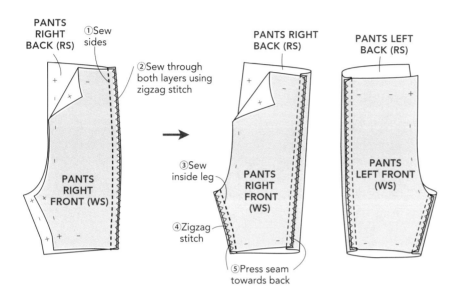

PANTS RIGHT BACK (RS)

①Sew sides

②Sew through both layers using zigzag stitch

PANTS RIGHT FRONT (WS)

PANTS RIGHT BACK (RS)

③Sew inside leg

④Zigzag stitch

PANTS RIGHT FRONT (WS)

⑤Press seam towards back

PANTS LEFT BACK (RS)

PANTS LEFT FRONT (WS)

2. Sew crotch

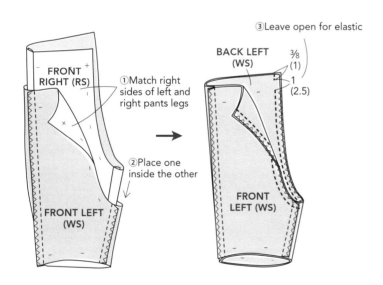

FRONT RIGHT (RS)

①Match right sides of left and right pants legs

②Place one inside the other

FRONT LEFT (WS)

③Leave open for elastic

BACK LEFT (WS)

⅜ (1)

1 (2.5)

FRONT LEFT (WS)

3. Create opening for elastic

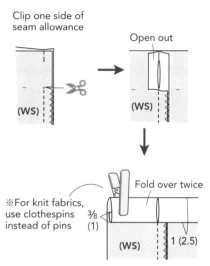

Clip one side of seam allowance

(WS)

Open out

(WS)

※For knit fabrics, use clothespins instead of pins

Fold over twice

⅜ (1)

1 (2.5)

(WS)

Sew

FRONT (RS)

4. Attach cuff trim

•Sew cuff trim into ring

①Divide pants cuff into four and mark sections

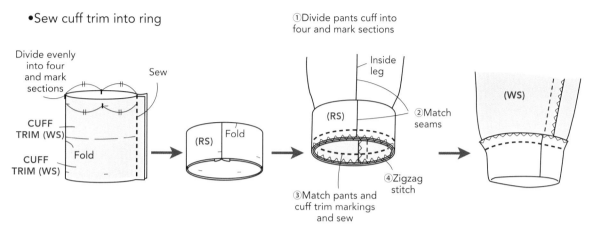

Divide evenly into four and mark sections

Sew

CUFF TRIM (WS)

CUFF TRIM (WS)

Fold

(RS) Fold

Inside leg

(RS)

②Match seams

④Zigzag stitch

③Match pants and cuff trim markings and sew

(WS)

5. Insert elastic

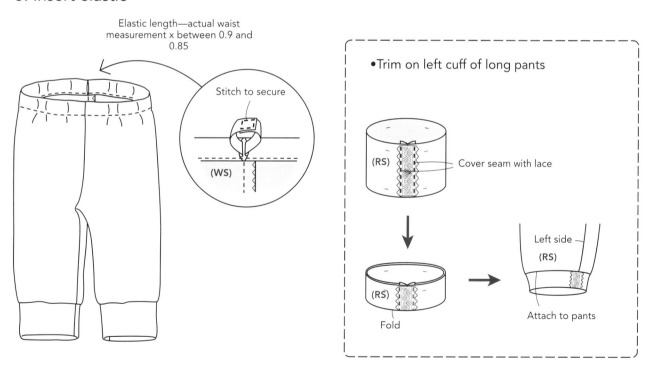

Elastic length—actual waist measurement x between 0.9 and 0.85

Stitch to secure

(WS)

•Trim on left cuff of long pants

(RS)

Cover seam with lace

(RS)

Fold

Left side

(RS)

Attach to pants

p. 18
Long-sleeve Coat in Knit Fabric

[materials]

※ Amount of fabric needed is listed from left to correspond to sizes 1-2 (90)/3-4 (100)/5-6 (110)/7-8 (120).

• Use needle and thread specifically for knits (see p 37)

• Main fabric—beige embroidered knit (light cotton knit) 45 in (110cm) wide—40/45/45/52 in (100/110/110/130cm)

• Adhesive interfacing for knits—8 in (20cm) x 20/20/24/24 in (50/50/60/60cm)

• Stay tape ½ in (1.2cm) wide—12 in (30cm)

• Buttons ½ in (1.2cm) diameter x 5 (for all sizes)

• Elastic 0.5cm wide—16 in (40cm)

★ Full-size pattern pieces are on side B of the pull-out page at the end of the book (※ draft pocket binding directly onto fabric as per measurements in cutting layout)

[sewing steps]

※ After cutting fabric, attach stay tape to shoulder seam allowance of front yoke and adhesive interfacing to wrong side of front placket.

1. Create gathering in body pieces, sew yokes to body pieces (see p 58).

2. Sew shoulders.

3. Attach sleeves to armholes.

4. Leaving an opening to pass elastic through, sew undersides of sleeves and sides in a continuous seam.

5. Sew cuffs and create opening for elastic.

6. Create pockets and attach to coat (see p 55).

7. Attach placket.

8. Create hood and attach to coat.

9. Fold hem up twice and sew.

10. Create buttonholes and attach buttons. Insert elastic through cuffs and stitch to secure.

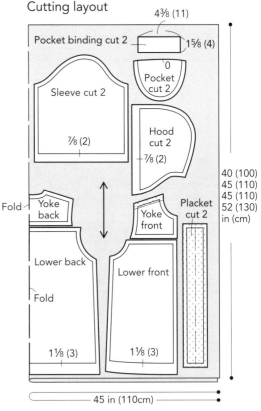

Cutting layout

Pocket binding cut 2 — 4⅜ (11) — 1⅝ (4)

Sleeve cut 2 — ⅞ (2)

Pocket cut 2 — 0

Hood cut 2 — ⅞ (2)

40 (100)
45 (110)
45 (110)
52 (130)
in (cm)

Fold — Yoke back

Yoke front

Placket cut 2

Lower back — Fold — 1⅛ (3)

Lower front — 1⅛ (3)

45 in (110cm)

※ All seam allowances ⅜ in (1cm) unless otherwise indicated
※ Amount of fabric required is given from top down as per sizes 1-2 (90)/3-4 (100)/5-6 (110)/7-8 (120)
▨ Attach adhesive interfacing to areas shaded in dots

1. Create gathers in body section and attach to yoke (see p 58)

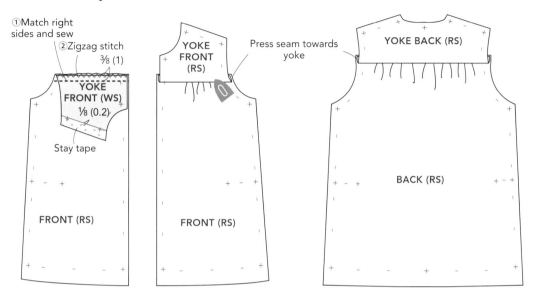

①Match right sides and sew

②Zigzag stitch
⅜ (1)

YOKE FRONT (WS)
⅛ (0.2)

Stay tape

FRONT (RS)

YOKE FRONT (RS)

Press seam towards yoke

FRONT (RS)

YOKE BACK (RS)

BACK (RS)

2. Sew shoulders

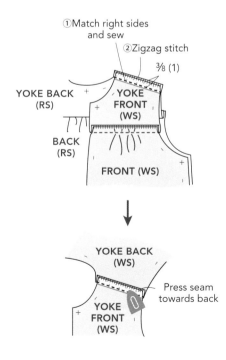

①Match right sides and sew

②Zigzag stitch
⅜ (1)

YOKE BACK (RS)

YOKE FRONT (WS)

BACK (RS)

FRONT (WS)

YOKE BACK (WS)

YOKE FRONT (WS)

Press seam towards back

3. Attach sleeves to armholes

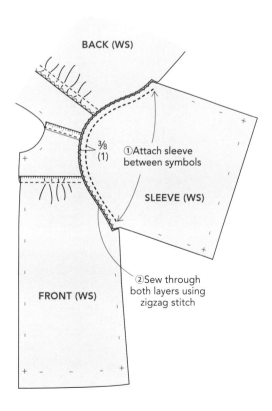

BACK (WS)

⅜ (1)

①Attach sleeve between symbols

SLEEVE (WS)

②Sew through both layers using zigzag stitch

FRONT (WS)

4. Sew undersides of sleeves and sides in a continuous seam

5. Create cuffs

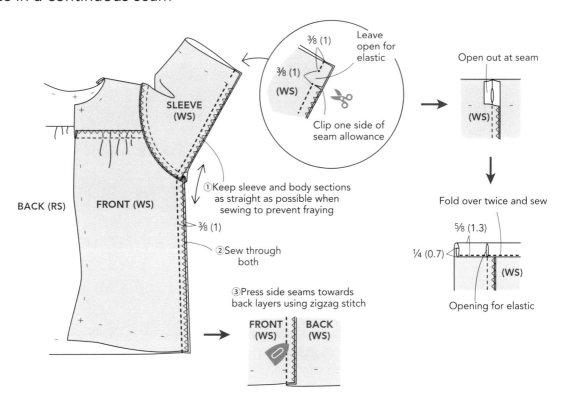

③Press side seams towards back layers using zigzag stitch

6. Create pockets and attach to garment (see p 55)

7. Attach placket

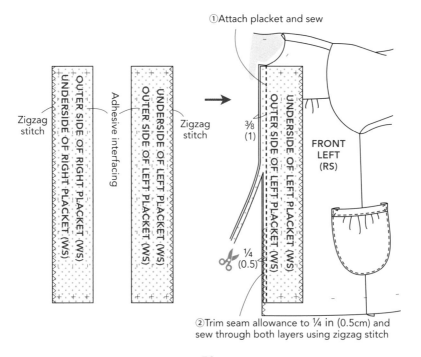

8. Create hood and attach to garment

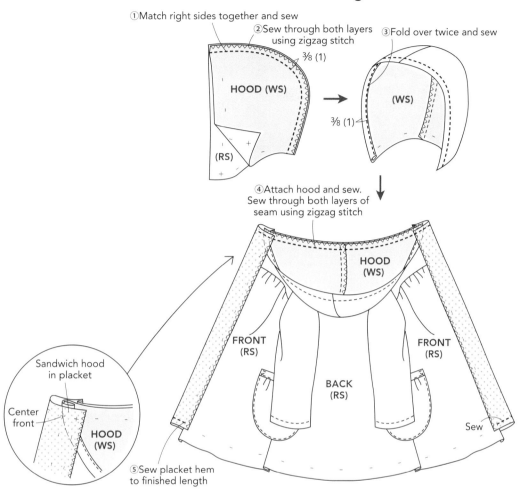

① Match right sides together and sew

② Sew through both layers using zigzag stitch

3/8 (1)

③ Fold over twice and sew

HOOD (WS)

(RS)

(WS)

3/8 (1)

④ Attach hood and sew. Sew through both layers of seam using zigzag stitch

HOOD (WS)

FRONT (RS)

FRONT (RS)

BACK (RS)

Sew

Sandwich hood in placket

Center front

HOOD (WS)

⑤ Sew placket hem to finished length

9. Sew hem and finish placket

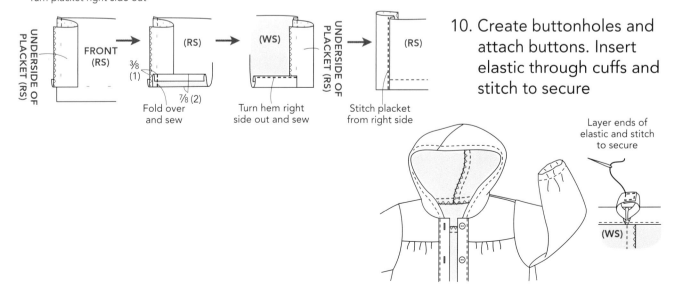

Turn placket right side out

UNDERSIDE OF PLACKET (RS)

FRONT (RS)

3/8 (1)

Fold over and sew

7/8 (2)

(RS)

(WS)

Turn hem right side out and sew

UNDERSIDE OF PLACKET (RS)

(RS)

Stitch placket from right side

10. Create buttonholes and attach buttons. Insert elastic through cuffs and stitch to secure

Layer ends of elastic and stitch to secure

(WS)

S p. 26
Short-sleeve Blouse with Round Collar

[materials]

※ Amount of fabric needed is listed from left to correspond to sizes 1-2 (90)/3-4 (100)/5-6 (110)/7-8 (120).

★ Use needle and thread specifically for knits (see p 37).

• Main fabric—knit of unbleached dots on gray ground (light cotton knit) 45 in (110cm) wide—36/36/40/40 in (90/90/100/100cm)

• Adhesive interfacing for knits 36 in (90cm) wide—16/16/16/20 in (40/40/40/50cm)

• Stay tape ½ in (1.2cm) wide—12 in (30cm)

• Buttons, ⅝ in (1.5cm) diameter x 2 in (5cm) (for all sizes)

• Elastic ¼ in (0.5cm) wide—16 in (40cm)

★ Full-size pattern pieces are on side B of the pull-out page at the end of the book (※draft hem trim directly onto fabric as per measurements in cutting layout)

[sewing steps]

※After cutting fabric, attach stay tape to shoulder seam allowance of front yoke and adhesive interfacing to wrong sides of front placket and outer collar.

1-5. Create as per long-sleeve knit coat (see p 69-70).

6. Attach binding to hem.

7. Attach front placket.

8. Create collar.

9. Attach collar and finish off placket.

10. Create buttonholes and attach buttons. Insert elastic through cuffs and stitch to secure (see p 71).

Cutting layout

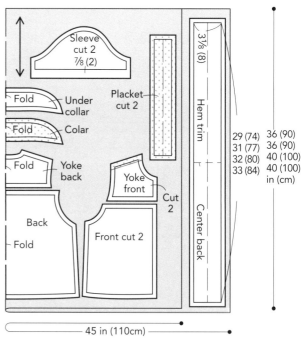

※All seam allowances ⅜ in (1cm) unless otherwise indicated
※Amount of fabric required is given from top down as per sizes 1-2 (90)/3-4 (100)/5-6 (110)/7-8 (120)
░░░Attach adhesive interfacing to areas shaded in dots

6. Attach trim to hem

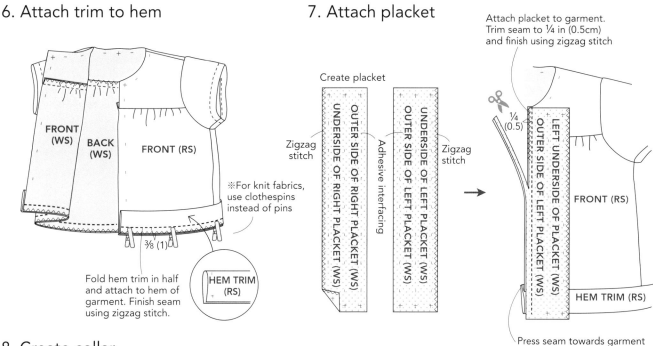

FRONT (WS)
BACK (WS)
FRONT (RS)

※For knit fabrics, use clothespins instead of pins

⅜ (1)

Fold hem trim in half and attach to hem of garment. Finish seam using zigzag stitch.

HEM TRIM (RS)

7. Attach placket

Create placket

UNDERSIDE OF RIGHT PLACKET (WS)
OUTER SIDE OF RIGHT PLACKET (WS)

Zigzag stitch

Adhesive interfacing

UNDERSIDE OF LEFT PLACKET (WS)
OUTER SIDE OF LEFT PLACKET (WS)

Zigzag stitch

Attach placket to garment. Trim seam to ¼ in (0.5cm) and finish using zigzag stitch

¼ (0.5)

LEFT UNDERSIDE OF PLACKET (WS)
OUTER SIDE OF LEFT PLACKET (WS)

FRONT (RS)

HEM TRIM (RS)

Press seam towards garment

8. Create collar

①Cut collar and under collar to the same measurements and match right sides together. Move collar seam so it lies ⅛ in (0.2cm) inside edge of under collar and sew.

UNDER COLLAR (RS)
⅜ (1)

②Trim seam

COLLAR (WS)

¼ (0.5)

Apply adhesive interfacing to wrong side of collar

⅛ (0.2)
COLLAR (RS)

③Turn to right side and press into shape. Stitch around outer edge.

Iron so seam is just inside edge of under collar

COLLAR (RS)

Align

9. Attach collar and finish placket

①Attach collar by sandwiching between edges of placket and sewing. Finish seam using zigzag stitch.

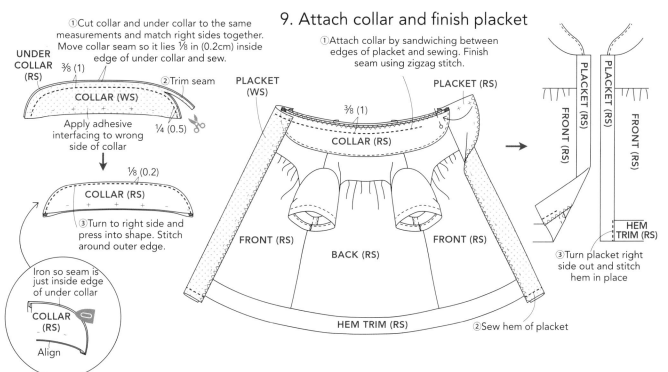

PLACKET (WS)

⅜ (1)

COLLAR (RS)

PLACKET (RS)

FRONT (RS)

BACK (RS)

FRONT (RS)

HEM TRIM (RS)

②Sew hem of placket

PLACKET (RS)
FRONT (RS)

PLACKET (RS)
FRONT (RS)

HEM TRIM (RS)

③Turn placket right side out and stitch hem in place

10. Attach buttons, insert elastic through cuffs and secure (see p 71)

(see p 71)

q p. 24
Neat Blouse

[materials]

※ Amount of fabric needed is listed from left to correspond to sizes 1-2 (90)/3-4 (100)/5-6 (110)/7-8 (120).

• Main fabric—plain white lawn
45 in (110cm) wide—32/32/32/36 in (80/80/80/90cm)

• Adhesive interfacing
36 in (90cm) wide—20 in (50cm)

• Buttons, ⅜ in (1cm) diameter, self-cover type x 5 (for back of garment)

★ Full-size pattern pieces are on side B of the pull-out page at the end of the book

[sewing steps]

※ After cutting out fabric, apply adhesive interfacing to wrong sides of outer collar, cuffs, and front and back facings.

1. Sew tucks in front yoke, attach decorative front placket.

2. Sew front yoke and front body sections together. Press seam towards yoke.

3. Sew shoulder seams and press seams towards back.

4. Sew front and back facings together at shoulders. Open out seams and finish off using zigzag stitch.

5. Create collar and baste to neckline.

6. Sew facings to blouse.

7. On sleeve pieces, create gathering at shoulders and attach to body sections. Press seams towards body sections.

8. Sew underside of sleeves and sides in a continuous seam. Press seams towards back.

9. Attach cuffs to sleeves.

10. Fold hem up twice and sew.

11. Create buttonholes at back and attach buttons. Attach decorative buttons to front.

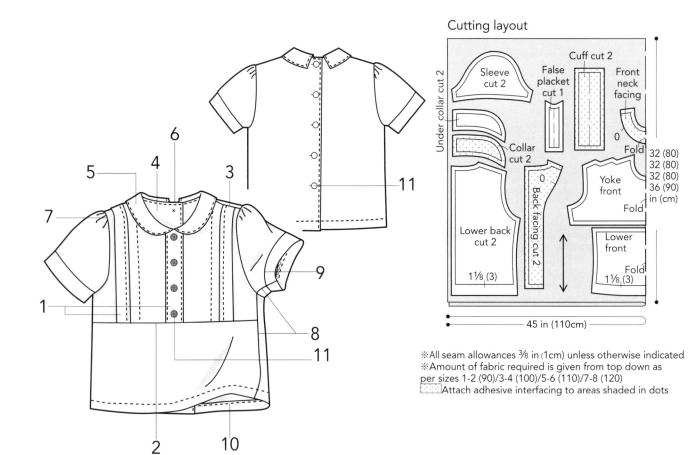

Cutting layout

Under collar cut 2

Sleeve cut 2

False placket cut 1

Cuff cut 2

Front neck facing

0

Collar cut 2

0

Back facing cut 2

Yoke front

Fold

Fold

32 (80)
32 (80)
32 (80)
36 (90)
in (cm)

Lower back cut 2

1⅛ (3)

Lower front

Fold

1⅛ (3)

45 in (110cm)

※All seam allowances ⅜ in (1cm) unless otherwise indicated
※Amount of fabric required is given from top down as per sizes 1-2 (90)/3-4 (100)/5-6 (110)/7-8 (120)
⸬⸬ Attach adhesive interfacing to areas shaded in dots

1. Sew front yoke, attach false placket

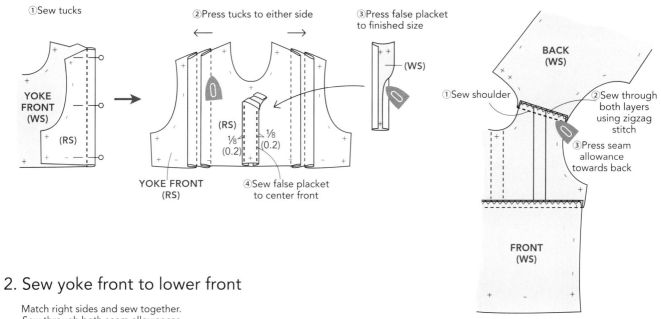

① Sew tucks

② Press tucks to either side

③ Press false placket to finished size

YOKE FRONT (WS)

(RS)

(RS)

(WS)

YOKE FRONT (RS)

(RS) $\frac{1}{8}$ (0.2) $\frac{1}{8}$ (0.2)

④ Sew false placket to center front

3. Sew shoulders

BACK (WS)

① Sew shoulder

② Sew through both layers using zigzag stitch

③ Press seam allowance towards back

FRONT (WS)

2. Sew yoke front to lower front

Match right sides and sew together. Sew through both seam allowances using zigzag stitch.

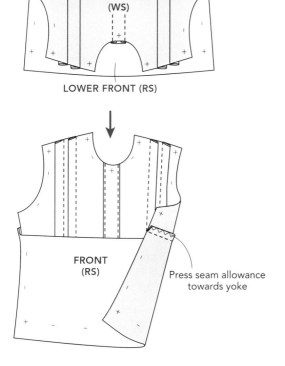

YOKE FRONT (WS)

LOWER FRONT (RS)

FRONT (RS)

Press seam allowance towards yoke

4. Sew facing

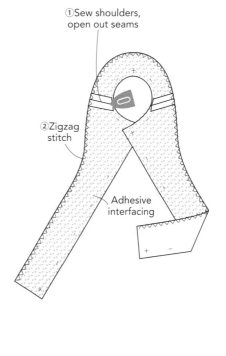

① Sew shoulders, open out seams

② Zigzag stitch

Adhesive interfacing

5. Create collar and baste to garment

Attach adhesive interfacing to wrong side of collar

Shift by ⅛ in (0.2cm)

UNDER COLLAR (RS)

⅛ (0.2)

⅛ (0.2)

COLLAR (WS)

COLLAR (WS)

①Cut collar and under collar to the same measurements and match right sides together. Move collar ⅛ in (0.2cm) towards inner edge and sew.

②Trim seam. Turn right side out and iron from under side. Stitch around edge. allowance to ¼ in (0.5cm)

Turn right side out and iron from under side. Stitch around edge.

⅛ (0.2)

⅛ (0.2)

COLLAR (RS)

COLLAR (RS)

Iron so seam is just inside edge of inner collar

UNDER COLLAR (RS)

Match edges

Baste to neckline

Center back

Center front

Center back

BACK (RS)

COLLAR (RS)

BACK (RS)

FRONT (RS)

6. Sew facing to garment

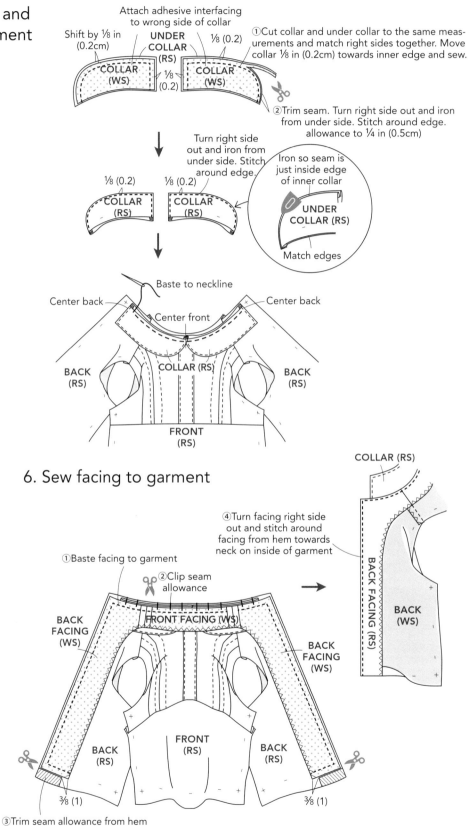

④Turn facing right side out and stitch around facing from hem towards neck on inside of garment

COLLAR (RS)

BACK FACING (RS)

BACK (WS)

①Baste facing to garment

②Clip seam allowance

BACK FACING (WS)

FRONT FACING (WS)

BACK FACING (WS)

BACK (RS)

FRONT (RS)

BACK (RS)

⅜ (1)

⅜ (1)

③Trim seam allowance from hem

76

7. Attach sleeves

Sew two rows of loose stitching either by hand or machine around shoulder section and pull up threads to gather

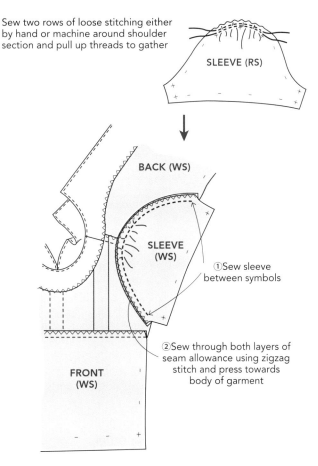

SLEEVE (RS)

BACK (WS)

SLEEVE (WS)

① Sew sleeve between symbols

② Sew through both layers of seam allowance using zigzag stitch and press towards body of garment

FRONT (WS)

8. Sew underside of sleeve and sides in a continuous seam

9. Attach cuffs to sleeves

10. Sew hem

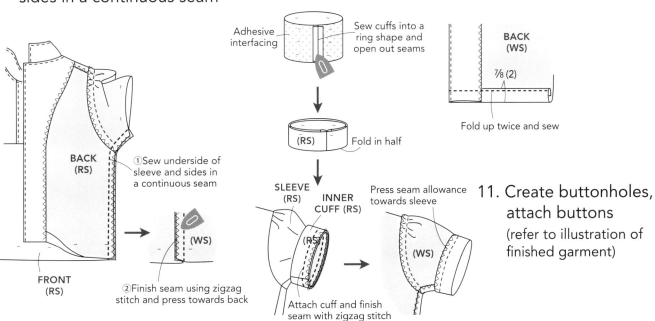

BACK (RS)

① Sew underside of sleeve and sides in a continuous seam

FRONT (RS)

(WS)

② Finish seam using zigzag stitch and press towards back

Adhesive interfacing

Sew cuffs into a ring shape and open out seams

(RS) Fold in half

SLEEVE (RS)

INNER CUFF (RS)

(RS)

Press seam allowance towards sleeve

(WS)

Attach cuff and finish seam with zigzag stitch

BACK (WS)

7/8 (2)

Fold up twice and sew

11. Create buttonholes, attach buttons
(refer to illustration of finished garment)

ρ p.23
Two Little Bags

[materials]

BAG A
- Fabric for main part of bag (including loop)—plain off-white 8¾ x 18 in (22 x 45cm)
- Other fabric (for pocket)—two types of striped fabric sewn together, 7 x 6½ in (18 x 16cm)
- Adhesive interfacing—16 x 20 in (40 x 50cm)
- Leather cord, ⅛ in (3mm wide)—brown x 40 in (1m) strips x 2

BAG B—WITH CROCHETED POCKET
- Fabric for main part of bag (including loop)—plain dark brown 8¾ x 18 in (22 x 45cm)
- Adhesive interfacing—8 x 20 in (20 x 50cm)
- Leather cord, ⅛ in (3mm wide)— green x 40 in (1m) strips x 3
- For pocket—unbleached cotton yarn, size 5/0 crochet hook

[sewing steps (for Bag A)]

1. Cut fabric out and apply adhesive interfacing to the wrong sides of the main fabric and the pocket piece.
2. Fold ends of the main bag piece and pocket piece twice and sew.
3. Create loop and baste to main bag piece.
4. Attach pocket.
5. Fold main bag piece and sew sides.
6. Turn bag to right side. Thread leather cord through loops and knot to keep in place.

[sewing steps (for Bag B)]

※ Create as for Bag A

★ Do not apply adhesive interfacing to pocket. Follow the crochet diagram to create a piece about 5¼ x 7 in (13 x 18cm) wide. When completed, thread green leather cord through edge of pocket and tie in place.

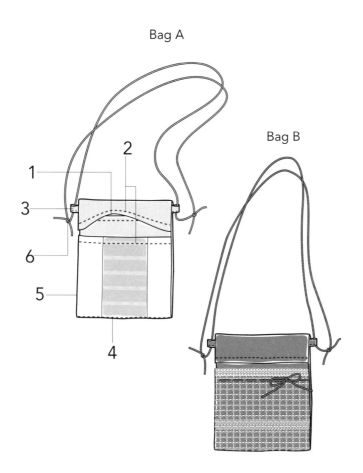

Bag A

Bag B

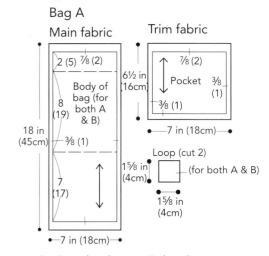

Bag A

Main fabric   Trim fabric

2 (5) ⅞ (2)
Body of bag (for both A & B)
6½ in (16cm)
⅞ (2)
Pocket
⅜ (1)
8 (19)
⅜ (1)
7 (18cm)
18 in (45cm)
⅜ (1)
1⅝ in (4cm)
Loop (cut 2)
(for both A & B)
7 (17)
1⅝ in (4cm)
7 in (18cm)

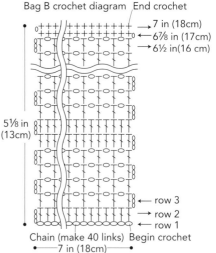

Bag B crochet diagram   End crochet

7 in (18cm)
6⅞ in (17cm)
6½ in (16 cm)
5⅛ in (13cm)
row 3
row 2
row 1
Chain (make 40 links) Begin crochet
7 in (18cm)

78

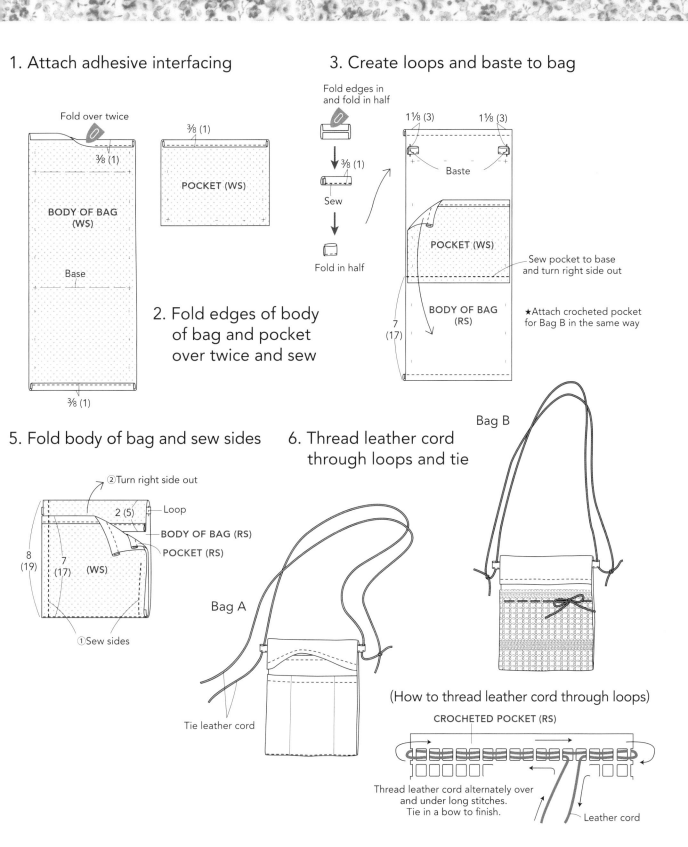

1. Attach adhesive interfacing

Fold over twice

⅜ (1)

BODY OF BAG (WS)

Base

⅜ (1)

⅜ (1)

POCKET (WS)

2. Fold edges of body of bag and pocket over twice and sew

3. Create loops and baste to bag

Fold edges in and fold in half

⅜ (1)

Sew

Fold in half

1⅛ (3)   1⅛ (3)

Baste

POCKET (WS)

Sew pocket to base and turn right side out

BODY OF BAG (RS)

7 (17)

★Attach crocheted pocket for Bag B in the same way

5. Fold body of bag and sew sides

②Turn right side out

2 (5) — Loop

BODY OF BAG (RS)

POCKET (RS)

8 (19)

7 (17)

(WS)

①Sew sides

6. Thread leather cord through loops and tie

Bag B

Bag A

Tie leather cord

(How to thread leather cord through loops)

CROCHETED POCKET (RS)

Thread leather cord alternately over and under long stitches.
Tie in a bow to finish.

Leather cord

Published in 2014 by Tuttle Publishing, an imprint of Periplus Editions (HK) Ltd.

www.tuttlepublishing.com

ISBN 978-4-8053-1308-4

Onnanoko no Oyofuku (NV6468)
Copyright © Yuki Araki/NIHON VOGUE-SHA 2007
English Translation © 2014 Periplus Editions (HK) Ltd.
Photographer: Shigeki Nakajima, Nobuo Suzuki (p. 14, 15)
Published through Japan UNI Agency, Inc. Tokyo
Translated from Japanese by Leeyong Soo

Distributed by

North America, Latin America & Europe

Tuttle Publishing
364 Innovation Drive,
North Clarendon,
VT 05759-9436 U.S.A.
Tel: 1 (802) 773-8930
Fax: 1 (802) 773-6993
info@tuttlepublishing.com
www.tuttlepublishing.com

Japan

Tuttle Publishing
Yaekari Building,
3rd Floor, 5-4-12 Osaki,
Shinagawa-ku,
Tokyo 141 0032
Tel: (81) 3 5437-0171
Fax: (81) 3 5437-0755
sales@tuttle.co.jp
www.tuttle.co.jp

Asia Pacific

Berkeley Books Pte. Ltd.
61 Tai Seng Avenue #02-12
Singapore 534167
Tel: (65) 6280-1330
Fax: (65) 6280-6290
inquiries@periplus.com.sg
www.periplus.com

Printed in Malaysia   1407TW
17 16 15 14   6 5 4 3 2 1

The Tuttle Story
"Books to Span the East and West"

Many people are surprised to learn that the world's largest publisher of books on Asia had its humble beginnings in the tiny American state of Vermont. The company's founder, Charles E. Tuttle, belonged to a New England family steeped in publishing.

Tuttle's father was a noted antiquarian dealer in Rutland, Vermont. Young Charles honed his knowledge of the trade working in the family bookstore, and later in the rare books section of Columbia University Library. His passion for beautiful books—old and new—never wavered throughout his long career as a bookseller and publisher.

After graduating from Harvard, Tuttle enlisted in the military and in 1945 was sent to Tokyo to work on General Douglas MacArthur's staff. He was tasked with helping to revive the Japanese publishing industry, which had been utterly devastated by the war. When his tour of duty was completed, he left the military, married a talented and beautiful singer, Reiko Chiba, and in 1948 began several successful business ventures.

To his astonishment, Tuttle discovered that postwar Tokyo was actually a book-lover's paradise. He befriended dealers in the Kanda district and began supplying rare Japanese editions to American libraries. He also imported American books to sell to the thousands of GIs stationed in Japan. By 1949, Tuttle's business was thriving, and he opened Tokyo's very first English-language bookstore in the Takashimaya Department Store in Ginza, to great success. Two years later, he began publishing books to fulfill the growing interest of foreigners in all things Asian.

Though a westerner, Tuttle was hugely instrumental in bringing a knowledge of Japan and Asia to a world hungry for information about the East. By the time of his death in 1993, he had published over 6,000 books on Asian culture, history and art—a legacy honored by Emperor Hirohito in 1983 with the "Order of the Sacred Treasure," the highest honor Japan can bestow upon a non-Japanese.

The Tuttle company today maintains an active backlist of some 1,500 titles, many of which have been continuously in print since the 1950s and 1960s—a great testament to Charles Tuttle's skill as a publisher. More than 60 years after its founding, Tuttle Publishing is more active today than at any time in its history, still inspired by Charles Tuttle's core mission—to publish fine books to span the East and West and provide a greater understanding of each.